DOMESDAY BOOK

Rutland

History from the Sources

DOMESDAY BOOK

A Survey of the Counties of England

LIBER DE WINTONIA

Compiled by direction of

KING WILLIAM I

Winchester
1086

DOMESDAY BOOK

general editor

JOHN MORRIS

29

Rutland

edited by

Frank Thorn

from a draft translation prepared by
Celia Parker

PHILLIMORE
Chichester
1980

1980
Published by
PHILLIMORE & CO. LTD.,
London and Chichester
Head Office: Shopwyke Hall,
Chichester, Sussex, England

ISBN 0 85033 173 0 (case)
ISBN 0 85033 174 9 (limp)

Printed in Great Britain by
Titus Wilson & Son Ltd.,
Kendal

RUTLAND

Introduction

The Domesday Survey of Rutland

History from the Sources
General Editor: John Morris

The series aims to publish history
written directly from the sources
for all interested readers, both
specialists and others. The first
priority is to publish important
texts which should be widely
available, but are not.

DOMESDAY BOOK

The contents, with the folio on which each county begins, are:

Domesday Book is termed *Liber de Wintonia* (The Book of Winchester) in column 332c

INTRODUCTION

The Domesday Survey

In 1066 Duke William of Normandy conquered England. He was crowned King, and most of the lands of the English nobility were soon granted to his followers. Domesday Book was compiled 20 years later. The Saxon Chronicle records that in 1085

> at Gloucester at midwinter ... the King had deep speech with his counsellors ... and sent men all over England to each shire ... to find out ... what or how much each landholder held ... in land and livestock, and what it was worth ... The returns were brought to him.[1]

William was thorough. One of his Counsellors reports that he also sent a second set of Commissioners 'to shires they did not know, where they were themselves unknown, to check their predecessors' survey, and report culprits to the King.'[2]

The information was collected at Winchester, corrected, abridged, chiefly by omission of livestock and the 1066 population, and fair-copied by one writer into a single volume. Norfolk, Suffolk and Essex were copied, by several writers, into a second volume, unabridged, which states that 'the Survey was made in 1086'. The surveys of Durham and Northumberland, and of several towns, including London, were not transcribed, and most of Cumberland and Westmorland, not yet in England, was not surveyed. The whole undertaking was completed at speed, in less than 12 months, though the fair-copying of the main volume may have taken a little longer. Both volumes are now preserved at the Public Record Office. Some versions of regional returns also survive. One of them, from Ely Abbey,[3] copies out the Commissioners' brief. They were to ask

> The name of the place. Who held it, before 1066, and now?
> How many hides?[4] How many ploughs, both those in lordship and the men's?
> How many villagers, cottagers and slaves, how many free men and Freemen?[5]
> How much woodland, meadow and pasture? How many mills and fishponds?
> How much has been added or taken away? What the total value was and is?
> How much each free man or Freeman had or has? All threefold, before 1066,
>   when King William gave it, and now; and if more can be had than at present?

The Ely volume also describes the procedure. The Commissioners took evidence on oath 'from the Sheriff; from all the barons and their Frenchmen; and from the whole Hundred, the priests, the reeves and six villagers from each village'. It also names four Frenchmen and four Englishmen from each Hundred, who were sworn to verify the detail.

The King wanted to know what he had, and who held it. The Commissioners therefore listed lands in dispute, for Domesday Book was not only a tax-assessment. To the King's grandson, Bishop Henry of Winchester, its purpose was that every 'man should know his right and not usurp another's'; and because it was the final authoritative register of rightful possession 'the natives called it Domesday Book, by analogy

---

[1] Before he left England for the last time, late in 1086. [2] Robert Losinga, Bishop of Hereford 1079-1095 (see *E.H.R.* 22, 1907, 74). [3] *Inquisitio Eliensis,* first paragraph. [4] A land unit, reckoned as 120 acres. [5] *Quot Sochemani.*

from the Day of Judgement'; that was why it was carefully arranged by Counties, and by landholders within Counties, 'numbered consecutively ... for easy reference'.6

Domesday Book describes Old English society under new management, in minute statistical detail. Foreign lords had taken over, but little else had yet changed. The chief landholders and those who held from them are named, and the rest of the population was counted. Most of them lived in villages, whose houses might be clustered together, or dispersed among their fields. Villages were grouped in administrative districts called Hundreds, which formed regions within Shires, or Counties, which survive today with minor boundary changes; the recent deformation of some ancient county identities is here disregarded, as are various short-lived modern changes. The local assemblies, though overshadowed by lords great and small, gave men a voice, which the Commissioners heeded. Very many holdings were described by the Norman term *manerium* (manor), greatly varied in size and structure, from tiny farmsteads to vast holdings; and many lords exercised their own jurisdiction and other rights, termed *soca*, whose meaning still eludes exact definition.

The Survey was unmatched in Europe for many centuries, the product of a sophisticated and experienced English administration, fully exploited by the Conqueror's commanding energy. But its unique assemblage of facts and figures has been hard to study, because the text has not been easily available, and abounds in technicalities. Investigation has therefore been chiefly confined to specialists; many questions cannot be tackled adequately without a cheap text and uniform translation available to a wider range of students, including local historians.

Previous Editions

The text has been printed once, in 1783, in an edition by Abraham Farley, probably of 1250 copies, at Government expense, said to have been £38,000; its preparation took 16 years. It was set in a specially designed type, here reproduced photographically, which was destroyed by fire in 1808. In 1811 and 1816 the Records Commissioners added an introduction, indices, and associated texts, edited by Sir Henry Ellis; and in 1861-1863 the Ordnance Survey issued zincograph facsimiles of the whole. Texts of individual counties have appeared since 1673, separate translations in the Victoria County Histories and elsewhere.

This Edition

Farley's text is used, because of its excellence, and because any worthy alternative would prove astronomically expensive. His text has been checked against the facsimile, and discrepancies observed have been verified against the manuscript, by the kindness of Miss Daphne Gifford of the Public Record Office. Farley's few errors are indicated in the notes.

6 *Dialogus de Scaccario* 1,16.

The editor is responsible for the translation and lay-out. It aims at what the compiler would have written if his language had been modern English; though no translation can be exact, for even a simple word like 'free' nowadays means freedom from different restrictions. Bishop Henry emphasized that his grandfather preferred 'ordinary words'; the nearest ordinary modern English is therefore chosen whenever possible. Words that are now obsolete, or have changed their meaning, are avoided, but measurements have to be transliterated, since their extent is often unknown or arguable, and varied regionally. The terse inventory form of the original has been retained, as have the ambiguities of the Latin.

Modern English commands two main devices unknown to 11th century Latin, standardised punctuation and paragraphs; in the Latin, *ibi* ('there are') often does duty for a modern full stop, *et* ('and') for a comma or semi-colon. The entries normally answer the Commissioners' questions, arranged in five main groups, (i) the place and its holder, its hides, ploughs and lordship; (ii) people; (iii) resources; (iv) value; and (v) additional notes. The groups are usually given as separate paragraphs.

King William numbered chapters 'for easy reference', and sections within chapters are commonly marked, usually by initial capitals, often edged in red. They are here numbered. Maps, indices and an explanation of technical terms are also given. Later, it is hoped to publish analytical and explanatory volumes, and associated texts.

The editor is deeply indebted to the advice of many scholars, too numerous to name, and especially to the Public Record Office, and to the publisher's patience. The draft translations are the work of a team; they have been co-ordinated and corrected by the editor, and each has been checked by several people. It is therefore hoped that mistakes may be fewer than in versions published by single fallible individuals. But it would be Utopian to hope that the translation is altogether free from error; the editor would like to be informed of mistakes observed.

The maps are the work of Jim Hardy and Frank Thorn.

The preparation of this volume has been greatly assisted by a generous grant from the Leverhulme Trust Fund.

This support, originally given to the late Dr. J. R. Morris, has been kindly extended to his successors. At the time of Dr. Morris's death in June 1977, he had completed volumes 2, 3, 11, 12, 19, 23, 24. He had more or less finished the preparation of volumes 13, 14, 20, 28. These and subsequent volumes in the series were brought out under the supervision of John Dodgson and Alison Hawkins, who have endeavoured to follow, as far as possible, the editorial principles established by John Morris.

Conventions

*   refers to a note to the Latin text

[ ]   enclose words omitted in the MS.   ( )   enclose editorial explanations.

In Rotelande.

.I. Rex.

.II. Judita comitiſſa.

.III. Roƀtus malet.

.IIII. Ogerius.

.V. Giſlebertus de gand.

.VI. Hugo comes.

.VII. Alƀtus clericus.

IN RUTLAND

ROTELAND.

293 c

In *ALFNODESTOV WAPENT* sunt . II . Hundrez.
In uno qq; . XII . carucatæ ad gld . 7 | In uno quoq; XXIIII . carucæ
esse . possunt . Hoc Wapentac dimid est in Turga
stune Wapentac . 7 dimid in Brochelestou Wapent.
In *MARTINESLEIE . WAP* . est . I . hundret . in quo
XII . caruc træ ad gld . 7 XL.VIII . carucæ . ee . possunt.
exceptis trib; dnicis regis Manerijs . in quib; pos
sunt arare XIIII . carucæ. ‸ geha ad gld regis.
H DVO WAPENT adjacent uicecomitatui Snotin
ROTELAND reddit regi . CL . libras albas.

ALFNODESTOV . WAPENTAC.

.I. M In *GRETHA* . hb Goda . III . car træ ad gld . Tra . VIII . car.
Ibi ht Rex . II . car in dnio . 7 XXXIII . uilt 7 IIII . bord.
hntes . VIII . car . 7 I . molin . 7 VII . acs pti . Silua p loca
past . XVI . qz lg . 7 VII . qz lat . T.R.E. ual . VII . lib
M In *COTESMORE* . hb Goda . III . car tre ‸ m . X . lib.
ad gld . Tra . XII . car . Ibi ht rex . III . car in dnio.
7 III . soch de dimid car huj træ . 7 XL . uilt 7 VI . bord
hntes . XX . car . Ibi . XL . ac pti . Silua una lev lg.
7 VII . qz lat . T.R.E . ual VII . lib . m X . lib.
De tra huj M ht qda Goisfrid dim carucata.
7 ibi ht . I . car . 7 VIII . uilt . Valet . XX . sol.

RUTLAND

R   In ALSTOE Wapentake
1   there are two Hundreds; in each 12 carucates taxable, and
in each 24 ploughs possible.
     Half of this Wapentake is in Thurgarton Wapentake, and
half is in Broxtow Wapentake.

     In MARTINSLEY Wapentake
2   there is one Hundred, and in it (are) 12 carucates of land
taxable, and 48 ploughs possible, apart from the King's
three lordship manors, in which 14 ploughs can plough.

3   These two Wapentakes are attached to the Sheriffdom of
Nottingham for the King's tax.

4   Rutland pays to the King £150, blanched.

     In ALSTOE Wapentake   (In the Northern Hundred)

1   [LAND OF THE KING]

5 M.   In GREETHAM Goda had 3 carucates of land taxable.
     Land for 8 ploughs. The King has 2 ploughs in lordship and
       33 villagers and 4 smallholders who have 8 ploughs.
       1 mill; meadow, 7 acres; woodland, pasture in places, 16
         furlongs long and 7 furlongs wide.
     Value before 1066 £7; now £10.

6 M.   In COTTESMORE Goda had 3 carucates of land taxable.
     Land for 12 ploughs. The King has 3 ploughs in lordship;
       3 Freemen with ½ carucate of this land; 40 villagers
         and 6 smallholders who have 20 ploughs.
       Meadow, 40 acres; woodland 1 league long and 7
         furlongs wide.
     Value before 1066 £7; now £10.
       One Geoffrey has ½ carucate of the land of this manor;
     he has 1 plough and
       8 villagers.
     Value 20s.

.II. ⊙ In OVERTVNE 7 Stratone ħƀ Wallef comes ^{BER'}

    III . car̄ træ 7 dim̄ ad glđ . Tra . XII . car̄ . Ibi ħr̄ Judita comitiſſa

    III . car̄ . 7 XXXV . uiłł 7 VIII . borđ . ħn̄tes . IX . car̄ . 7 XL . ac̄ p̄ti .

    Silua paſt p̄ loca . I . lev lḡ . 7 dim̄ lev lat . T.R.E . ual . XII .

    liƀ . m̊ . XX . liƀ . Alured cal̄uniat̄ . IIII . part̄ē in ſtratune . ^{de Lincole}

⊙ In TISTERTVNE ħƀ Erich dim̄ car̄ tre ad glđ . Tra . I . car̄ .

    Ibi Hugo de Judita ħr̄ . I . car̄ . 7 VI . uiłł cū . I . car̄ . T.R.E . ^{com̄}

    ual XX . ſoł . m̊ . XL . ſoł .

⊙ IBID E ħƀ Siuuard dim̄ car̄ træ ad glđ . Tra . I . car̄ .

.III.   Ibi Alured ħr̄ . I . car̄ . 7 III . uiłł . 7 II . borđ . cū dim̄ car̄ . ^{de Lincole 9}

    T.R.E . ual . XX . ſoł . m̊ LX . ſoł .

⊙ In eod hund ħƀ Goduin . I . car̄ træ 7 dim̄ ad glđ . T̄ra ^{In TIE}

.IIII.   V . car̄ . Ibi Roƀt malet ħr̄ . II . car̄ . 7 XV . uiłł cū . II . car̄ . ⁹

    p̄tū . IIII . q̄ʒ in lḡ . 7 III . q̄ʒ lat . Ibi . I . moliñ . II . ſolidoʒ .

.II. T.R.E . ual IIII . liƀ . m̊ ſimilit̄ .

2   **[LAND OF COUNTESS JUDITH]**

7 M. In (Market) OVERTON and its outlier, STRETTON, Earl Waltheof
      had 3½ carucates of land taxable. Land for 12 ploughs.
      Countess Judith has 3 ploughs and
          35 villagers and 8 smallholders who have 9 ploughs.
          Meadow, 40 acres; woodland, pasture in places, 1 league
            long and ½ league wide.
      Value before 1066 £12; now £20.   *(ELc 11)*
          Alfred of Lincoln claims a fourth part, in Stretton.

8 M. In THISTLETON Eric had ½ carucate of land taxable.
      Land for 1 plough. Hugh has from Countess Judith 1 plough and
          6 villagers with 1 plough.
      Value before 1066, 20s; now 40s.   *(ELc 12)*

[2a]   **[LAND OF ALFRED OF LINCOLN]**

9 M. There also Siward had ½ carucate of land taxable.
      Land for 1 plough. Alfred of Lincoln has 1 plough and
          3 villagers and 2 smallholders with ½ plough.
      Value before 1066, 20s; now 60s.   *(ELc 7)*

[3]   **[LAND OF ROBERT MALET]**

10 M. In the same Hundred in
      TEIGH Godwin had 1½ carucates of land taxable.
      Land for 5 ploughs. Robert Malet has 2 ploughs and
          15 villagers with 4 ploughs.
          Meadow 4 furlongs in length and 3 furlongs wide. 1 mill, 2s.
      Value before 1066 £4; now the same.

ꝏ In *WICHINGEDENE* . ħb Wallef . iiii . car̄ træ ad glđ.

Tra . xii . car̄ . Ibi Hugo de comitiſſa hꝉ . v . car̄ . 7 xxvii.

uiℓℓ 7 vi . borđ . hn̄tes . viii . car̄ . T.R.E. uaℓ . viii . liƀ . m̄

ꝏ In *EXENTVNE* ħb Wallef com̄ . ii . car̄ tre ad glđ ⌐xiii . liƀ.

Tra . xii . car̄ . Ibi hꝉ Judita . iii . car̄ . 7 xxxvii . uiℓℓ . cū

viii . car̄ . 7 ii . moliñ . xiii . foliđ . p̄tū . vi . q̄ᷓ in long.

293 d
Silua ꝑ loca paſt . v . q̄ᷓ ℓḡ . 7 v . laꞇ . T.R.E. uaℓ

viii . liƀ . m̄ . x . liƀ.

ꝏ In *WITEWELLE* . ħb Beſẏ . i . car̄ tre ad glđ . Tra

iii . car̄ . Ibi Herƀt de comitiſſa hꝉ . i . car̄ . 7 vi . uiℓℓ

7 iiii . borđ hn̄tes . ii . car̄ . Ibi æccℓa 7 pƀr . 7 xx . ac̄ p̄ti.

7 i . moliñ xii . den̄ . Silua ꝑ loca paſt . vi . q̄ᷓ 7 vi .

★ p̄tic in ℓḡ . 7 iii . q̄ᷓ 7 xiii . p̄tic in laꞇ . T.R.E. uaℓ xl.

ꝏ In *ALESTANESTORP* . ħb Leuric . i . car̄ ⌐ſoℓ . m̄ . xl.

træ ad glđ . Tra . v . car̄ . Ibi Oger̄ filius Vngemar

de rege hꝉ . ii . caꞃ . 7 xi . uiℓℓ 7 iiii . borđ . cū . iiii . car̄.

7 xvi . ac̄s p̄ti . Silua paſt . iii . q̄ᷓ ℓḡ . 7 ii . laꞇ . T.R.E.

7 m̄ uaℓ xl . foℓ.

(In the Southern Hundred)

[2]   [LAND OF COUNTESSS JUDITH]

11 2 In WHISSENDINE Earl Waltheof had 4 carucates of land taxable.
   M. Land for 12 ploughs. Hugh of Hotot has from the
Countess 5 ploughs and
      27 villagers and 6 smallholders who have 8 ploughs.
Value before 1066 £8; now £13.   (ELc 13)

12 M. In EXTON Earl Waltheof had 2 carucates of land taxable.
     Land for 12 ploughs. Countess Judith has 3 ploughs and
      37 villagers with 8 ploughs.
      2 mills, 13s; meadow 6 furlongs in length; woodland,
        pasture in places, 5 furlongs long and 5 wide.   293 d
Value before 1066 £8; now £10.   (ELc 14)

13 M. In WHITWELL Besi had 1 carucate of land taxable.
     Land for 3 ploughs. Herbert has from Countess
Judith 1 plough and
      6 villagers and 4 smallholders who have 2 ploughs.
      A church and a priest; meadow, 20 acres; 1 mill, 12d;
        woodland, pasture in places, 6 furlongs and 6 perches
        in length and 3 furlongs and 13 perches in width.
Value before 1066, 20s; now 40[s].   (ELc 15)

[4]   [LAND OF OGER]

14 M. In 'AWSTHORP' Leofric had 1 carucate of land taxable.
     Land for 5 ploughs. Oger son of Ungomar has from the
King 2 ploughs and
      11 villagers and 4 smallholders with 4 ploughs.
      Meadow, 16 acres; woodland pasture 3 furlongs long
       and 2 wide.
Value before 1066 and now 40s.

Ↄ̄ In *BVRGELAI* . ħƀ Vlf . ɪɪ . caꝛ́ træ ad glđ . Tra . vɪɪ .

caꝛ́ . Ibi Goisfriđ ħō Giſleƀti de gand ħt . ɪɪ . caꝛ́ .

7 xxx . uiłł 7 vɪɪɪ . borđ hñtes . ɪɪɪɪ . caꝛ́ . 7 xxx . acs p̄ti .

Silua p̱ loca past́ . ɪ . lev́ lḡ . 7 ɪɪɪ . q̃ꝫ laꝛ́ . T.R.E.

uał . ɪɪɪɪ . liƀ . m̊ . c . ſoł .

Ↄ̄ In *EꝂVVELLE* . ħƀ Harold᷑ . ɪɪ . caꝛ́ træ ad glđ .

Tra᷑ . vɪ . caꝛ́ . Ibi Gozelin᷑ ħō Hugonis ħt . ɪɪ . caꝛ́ .

7 xɪɪɪ . uiłł 7 ɪɪɪ . borđ . hñtes . v . caꝛ́ . 7 xvɪ . acs p̄ti .

T.R.E . uał . c . ſoł . m̊ . vɪ . liƀ .

MARTINESLEI WAPENTAC.

Ↄ̄ In *OCHEHA* . Chercheïoch . ħƀ Eddid regina . ɪɪɪɪ .

caꝛ́ træ ad glđ . Tra . xvɪ . caꝛ́ . Ibi ħt Rex . ɪɪ . caꝛ́

ad aulā . 7 tam aliæ . ɪɪɪɪ ꞏ poſſuꝕ . ee . Ibi ſuꝕ . cxxxvɪɪɪ .

uiłłi . 7 xɪx . borđ . hñtes xxxvɪɪ . caꝛ́ . 7 q̃t xx . ac̊

p̄ti . Ibi p̄ƀr 7 æccła . ad quā ptiñ . ɪɪɪɪ . bouatæ huj᷑ træ .

Silua paſtił . ɪ . lev́ lḡ . 7 dim̊ lev́ laꝛ́ . T.R.E . uał . xl . liƀ .

Ↄ̄ IBIDĒ ħƀ Leuenot . ɪ . caꝛ́ træ ad glđ . .

Fułcher ħt ibi . v . boꝉ in caꝛ́ . 7 vɪ . acs p̄ti . T.R.E . 7 m̊ . xx .

Toꝉ Ↄ̄ cū BEꝫ . ɪɪɪ . lev́ lḡ . 7 ɪ . lev́ 7 vɪɪɪ . q̃ꝫ laꝛ́ .

[5]   [LAND OF GILBERT OF GHENT]

15 M. In BURLEY Ulf had 2 carucates of land taxable.
Land for 7 ploughs. Geoffrey, Gilbert of Ghent's man,
has 2 ploughs and
30 villagers and 8 smallholders who have 4 ploughs.
Meadow, 30 acres; woodland, pasture in places, 1 league
long and 3 furlongs wide.
Value before 1066 £4; now 100s.   *(ELc 5)*

[6]   [LAND OF EARL HUGH]

16 M. In ASHWELL Earl Harold had 2 carucates of land taxable.
Land for 6 ploughs. Jocelyn, Earl Hugh's man,
has 2 ploughs and
13 villagers and 3 smallholders who have 5 ploughs.
Meadow, 16 acres.
Value before 1066, 100s; now £6.   *(ELc 4)*

In MARTINSLEY Wapentake

[1]   [LAND OF THE KING]

17 M. In OAKHAM, with 5 outliers, Church jurisdiction, Queen Edith
had 4 carucates of land taxable. Land for 16 ploughs.
The King has 2 ploughs at the hall; however, another 4 ploughs
possible.
138 villagers and 19 smallholders who have 37 ploughs.
Meadow, 80 acres.
A priest and a church to which 4 bovates of this
land belong; woodland pasture 1 league long
and ½ league wide.
Value before 1066 £40.

18 M. There also Leofnoth had 1 carucate of land taxable.
Fulchere Malsor has 5 oxen in a plough and
meadow, 6 acres.
[Value] before 1066 and now, 20s.
The whole manor, with the outliers, 3 leagues long and 1
league and 8 furlongs wide.

ꝣIn _HAMELDVNE_ Cherchefoch. ħƀ Eddid. iiii. caȓ tre
ad glđ. Tra. xvi. caȓ. Ibi ħȓ Rex. v. caȓ. in dñio.7 cxl.
uiłłos.7 xiii. borđ. ħntes xl. caȓ. Ibi. iii. pƀri.7 iii. æcclæ
ubi ꝑtiñ. i. bou 7 viii. ac tre. Ibi. i. moliñ xxi. foliđ
7 iiii. den.7 xl. ac ꝑti. Silua minuta fertił ꝑ loca. iii.
lev łg.7 i. lev 7 dim lat. T.R.E. uał.l.ii. liƀ.

Toȶ ꝳ cu Beȝ. iii. lev 7 viii. q̇ȝ łg.7 ii. lev 7 viii. q̇ȝ lat.

ꝣIn _REDLINCTVNE_ Cherchefoch ħƀ Eddid. iiii. caȓ træ
ad glđ. Tra. xvi. caȓ. Ibi ħȓ rex. iiii. caȓ. in dñio.7 clxx.
uiłłos.7 xxvi. borđ. ħntes xxx. caȓ.7 ii. focħ cu. ii. caȓ.
Ibi. ii. pƀri.7 iii. æcclæ.7 ii. fed moliñ.7 xl. ac ꝑti. Silua
ꝑ loca paſt. ii. lev łg.7 viii. q̇ȝ lat. T.R.E. uał. xl. liƀ.
Totu ꝳ cu Beȝ. iii. lev 7 vii. q̇ȝ łg.7 ii. lev 7 ii. q̇ȝ lat.

294 a

In ꝑdicta tra ħȓ Alƀȓ cleric. i. bou træ.7 ibi ħȓ
.i. moliñ. xvi. denaȓ. Æcclam q̇q̇ de Ocheħa 7 de
Hameldun.7 Ꞩ Petri de ſtanford q̇ ꝑtiñ ad Hamelđ
cu adjacentibȝ tris eifđe æccliis. hoc.ē. vii. bouatiſ.
ħȓ ifđe Alƀtus de rege. In ead ej tra poſſunt
ee. viii. carucæ.7 tam ibi araꞃ. xvi. carucæ.

Ipfe ħȓ ibi in dñio. iiii. caȓ.7 xviii. uiłł 7 vi. borđ
ħntes. v. caȓ.

T.R.E. uał. viii. liƀ. m̂. x. liƀ.

19 M. In HAMBLETON, with 7 outliers, Church jurisdiction, Queen
Edith had 4 carucates of land taxable. Land for 16 ploughs.
The King has 5 ploughs in lordship, and
140 villagers and 13 smallholders who have 40 ploughs.
3 priests and 3 churches, where 1 bovate and 8 acres of
land belong. 1 mill, 21s 4d; meadow, 40 acres;
underwood, fertile in places, 3 leagues long and 1½ leagues wide.
Value before 1066 £52.
The whole manor, with the outliers, 3 leagues and 8 furlongs
long and 2 leagues and 8 furlongs wide.

20 M. In RIDLINGTON, with 7 outliers, Church jurisdiction, Queen
Edith had 4 carucates of land taxable. Land for 16 ploughs.
The King has 4 ploughs in lordship, and
170 villagers and 26 smallholders who have 30 ploughs;
2 Freemen with 2 ploughs.
2 priests and 3 churches; 2 mill-sites; meadow, 40 acres;
woodland, pasture in places, 2 leagues long and
8 furlongs wide.
Value before 1066 £40.
The whole manor, with the outliers, 3 leagues and 7 furlongs
long and 2 leagues and 2 furlongs wide.

[7]   [LAND OF ALBERT THE CLERK]

21   In the aforesaid land Albert the Clerk has 1 bovate   294 a
of land, he has 1 mill, 16d.
Albert also has from the King the church of Oakham,
of Hambleton, and St. Peter's of Stamford, which belongs
to Hambleton, with the attached lands of these churches,
that is 7 bovates. In this land of his, 8 ploughs possible;
however, 16 ploughs plough there.
He has in lordship 4 ploughs and
18 villagers and 6 smallholders who have 5 ploughs.
Value before 1066 £8; now £10.

TERRA REGIS *IN WICESLEA WAPENT̃.*

Rex ten̄ *CHETENE* . Ibi funt . VII . hidæ . Tra . ē XIII . car̄

In dn̄io funt . II . 7 III . ferui . 7 XII . fochemans 7 XXIIII . uilt 7 v.

bord cū p̃bro hn̄tes . XI . car . Ibi molin̄ de . VI . fot 7 VIII . den̄.

7 XL . ac̄ p̃ti . Siluæ uilis . XVI . ac̄.

Huic m̃ ptin̄ *TICHESOVRE* . Ibi funt . II . hidæ . Tra . ē . VIII . car̄.

Ibi . XVI . fochm cū . IIII . bord hn̄t . VI . car̄ . Ibi molin̄ de . V . fot.

7 VIII . ac̄ p̃ti . 7 III . ac̄ fpineti.

Tot̄ T.R.E. ualb̄ . c . fot . Modo . x . lib̄.

Rex ten̄ *BERCHEDONE* . Ibi funt . IIII . hidæ una v min̄ . Tra . ē . x.

car̄ . Ibi funt . IX . uitti 7 x . fochi cū . III . bord hn̄tes . VI . car̄ 7 dim̄.

Ibi . XVI . ac̄ p̃ti . 7 VI . ac̄ fpineti . Huic m̃ ptin̄ t̄ mēbra.

In *SEIETON* . I . hida 7 dimiđ 7 I . bouata træ . Tra . ē . VI . car̄ 7 II . ac̄ p̃ti.

In *TORP* . una hida 7 una v træ . Tra . ē . IIII . car̄ . 7 III . ac̄ p̃ti.

In *MORCOTE* . IIII . hidæ . Tra . ē VIII . car̄ . 7 VI . ac̄ p̃ti.

In *BITLESBROCH* 7 *GLADESTONE* I . hida 7 dim̄ . Tra ē . IIII . car̄ . 7 VIII . ac̄ p̃ti.

In *LVFENHAM* . IIII . hidæ . Tra . ē . x . car̄ . 7 XVI . ac̄ p̃ti.

In his tris funt . XV . fochi 7 XXXIII . uitti 7 XXIII . bord cū p̃bro

hn̄tes . XIX . car̄ . In Seietone . ē molin̄ de XXXVI . den̄ . Silua

⋆ una q̃z̃ lg̃ 7 una lat̄ . Spinetū . 7 VI . q̃z̃ lg̃ . 7 II . q̃z̃ lat̄.

Tot̄ T.R.E. ualb̄ . III . lib̄ . Modo . VII . lib̄.

Rutland Holdings entered under other Counties

EN   ## NORTHAMPTONSHIRE

1   ### LAND OF THE KING   219 b

In WITCHLEY Wapentake

EN1 1 The King holds KETTON. 7 hides. Land for 13 ploughs.
   In lordship 2; 3 slaves;
      12 Freemen, 24 villagers and 5 smallholders with a priest
      who have 11 ploughs.
   A mill at 6s 8d; meadow, 40 acres; poor woodland, 16 acres.

   TIXOVER belongs to this manor. 2 hides. Land for 8 ploughs.
      16 Freemen with 4 smallholders have 6 ploughs.
   A mill at 5s; meadow, 8 acres; spinney, 3 acres.
   Value of the whole before 1066, 100s; now £10.

EN2 2a The King holds BARROWDEN. 4 hides, less 1 virgate.
   Land for 10 ploughs.
      9 villagers and 10 Freemen with 3 smallholders
      who have 6½ ploughs.
   Meadow, 16 acres; spinney, 6 acres.
   To this manor belong these members:-
   b In SEATON 1½ hides and 1 bovate of land. Land for 6 ploughs.
      Meadow, 4 acres.
   c In THORPE (by Water) 1 hide and 1 virgate of land. Land for 4 ploughs.
      Meadow, 3 acres.
   d In MORCOTT 4 hides. Land for 8 ploughs. Meadow, 6 acres.
   e In BISBROOKE and GLASTON 1½ hides. Land for 4 ploughs.
      Meadow, 8 acres.
   f In LUFFENHAM 4 hides. Land for 10 ploughs. Meadow, 16 acres.
   g In these lands are 15 Freemen, 33 villagers and 23 smallholders
      with a priest who have 19 ploughs.
      In SEATON a mill at 36d; woodland 1 furlong long and 1 wide;
         spinney, 6 furlongs long and 2 furlongs wide.
   Value of the whole before 1066 £3; now £7.

Rex ten *Lvfenha* 7 *Scvletorp*. Ibi funt . vii . hidæ 7 una v træ

Trā . ē . xiiii . car̄ . Ibi funt . xii . fochi 7 xvi . bord̄ cū p̄bro

hn̄tes . xii . car̄ . Ibi . ii . molini de xl . den̄ . 7 x . ac̄ p̄ti.

T.R.E . ualb̄ . xxx . fol . Modo . lx . folid̄ . Hōēs opant̄ opa regis

quæ p̄pofitus juſſerit.   ⌐de rege.

Has tras tenuit regina Eddid̄ . Modo ten̄ Hugo de porth ad firmā

Rex ten̄ *Castretone*. Mōrcar tenuit . Ibi funt . iii . hidæ

7 dim̄ . Tra . ē . ix . car̄ . In dn̄io . ē una . 7 xxiiii . uiłłi 7 ii . fochi

7 ii . bord̄ cū p̄bro 7 ii . feruis hn̄t . vii . car̄ . Ibi molin̄ de . xvi.

folid̄ . 7 xvi . ac̄ p̄ti . Spinetū . iii . q̄ 7 lḡ . 7 ii . q̄ lat̄ . ⌐de rege.

Valuit . vi . lib̄ . Modo . x . lib̄ . Hugo . f . baldric ten̄ ad firmā

Rex ht̄ in dn̄io de Portland . ii . carucatas . 7 ii . partes tciæ

carucatæ . 7 xii . ac̄s p̄ti . Ad æcclam S̄ Petri jacet . i . car̄ træ.

7 ad æcclam ōmiū scōʒ dimid̄ carucata . Portland cū p̄to T.R.E.

reddeb̄ xl . viii . fol . 7 x . folid̄ p̄ feltris fōmarioʒ regis.

Sup hæc deber rex habe . ix . lib̄ 7 xii . fol . p̄ aliis exitib̄ burgi.

.III. TERRA EP̄I DVNELMENSIS. *In Wiceslea Wapent.*

Ep̄s Dvnelmensis ten̄ . ii . hid̄ de rege in *Horne* . Tra . iiii . car̄.

Nc̄ in dn̄io . i . car̄ . 7 xii . uiłłi cū p̄bro 7 i . focho 7 vii . bord̄ 7 i . feruo . hn̄t

iiii . car̄ . Ibi . iii . molin̄i de . xx . folid̄ . Silua . i . q̄ 7 xii . ptic̄ lḡ . 7 xvii . ptic̄

lat̄ . Valuit 7 ual . iiii . lib̄ . Langfer tenuit de rege . E . cū faca 7 foca.

EN3 3 The King holds LUFFENHAM and 'SCULTHORP'. 7 hides and 1
virgate of land. Land for 14 ploughs.
  12 Freemen and 16 smallholders with a priest who
    have 12 ploughs.
  2 mills at 40d; meadow, 10 acres.
Value before 1066, 30s; now 60s.
The men perform the King's work as the reeve orders.
Queen Edith held these lands. Now Hugh of Port holds them
from the King at a revenue.

EN4 4 The King holds CASTERTON. Earl Morcar held it. 3½ hides.   219 c
Land for 9 ploughs. In lordship 1.
  24 villagers, 2 Freemen and 2 smallholders with a priest
    and 2 slaves have 7 ploughs.
  A mill at 16s; meadow, 16 acres; spinney 3 furlongs long
    and 2 furlongs wide.
The value was £6; now £10.
Hugh son of Baldric holds it from the King at a revenue.

EN5 5 In the lordship of ?ORTLAND the King has 2 carucates
and 2 parts of a third carucate and
  meadow, 12 acres.
  1 carucate of land lies with (the lands of) St. Peter's
    Church, and ½ carucate with All Saints' Church.
Portland with the meadow, paid 48s before 1066, and 10s
for horse-cloths for the King's packhorses. In addition the
King ought to have £9 12s from the other income of the Borough.

3   LAND OF THE BISHOP OF DURHAM   220 b

In WITCHLEY Wapentake
EN6 1 The Bishop of Durham holds 2 hides from the King in HORN.
Land for 4 ploughs. Now in lordship 1 plough.
  12 villagers with a priest, 1 Freeman, 7 smallholders and
    1 slave have 4 ploughs.
  3 mills at 20s; woodland 1 furlong and 12 perches long
    and 17 perches wide.
The value was and is £4.
  Langfer held it from King Edward, with full jurisdiction.

221 a

.V. TERRA EPI LINCOLIENSIS.

De ipſo epo ten̄ Walteriꝰ. II . hiđ in *LIDENTONE*.

Ibi ptin̄ *STOCHE*. Smeliſtone. Caldecote. Tra̷.ē. XVI.

car̄ int totū. In dn̄io ſunt. VI . car̄. 7 IIII . ſerui. 7 XXVI.

uilti 7 XXIIII. borđ hn̄tes. IX . car̄. Ibi . II . molini de . VIII.

ſoliđ. 7 XXVIII. ac̄ pti. Silua . III . q̄rent̷ lḡ. 7 II . q̷ laī.

Valet toī . VIII . liḃ. Bardi tenuit cū ſaca 7 ſoca.

De eođ epo ten̄ Walteriꝰ. I . hiđ in *ESINDONE*. Tra̷.ē

VI. car̄. In dn̄io ſūnt . II . cū . I . ſeruo. 7 XVI . uilti 7 V . borđ

cū . IIII. car̄. Ibi molin̄ de . XVI. ſoliđ. 7 III . ac̄ pti.

Silua . VI. q̷ lḡ. 7 IIII. q̄rent̷ laī. Valuit . IIII . liḃ.

Modo . c . ſoliđ. Bardi tenuit cū ſaca 7 ſoca.

221 b

.VI. TERRA SC̄I PETRI DE BVRG.

Ipſa æccła ten̄ . VI. hiđ in *VNDELE*. Tra̷.ē. IX. car̄. In dn̄io ſuꬷ

III . car̄. 7 III. ſerui. 7 XXIII. uilti 7 X. borđ cū. IX. car̄. Ibi molin̄

de. XX. ſoī. 7 CC.L. anguill. 7 ibi . L. ac̄ pti. Silua . III. leū lḡ.

7 II . leū lat. Cū onerat̄. ual̄. XX. ſoī. De mercato. XXV. ſoī.

Valuit. V . ſoī. Modo . XI . liḃ.

Huic m̄ ptin̄ dimiđ hida in Terninge. Tra̷.ē dim̄ car̄. Ibi . ē

un̄ uilts. Valuit. II. ſoī. Modo. XL. denar̄. *IN WICESLE HVNĐ*

Ipſi m̄ ptin̄. II. hidæ 7 una v̄ træ.in *STOCHE*. Tra̷.ē. VIII. car̄.

221 c

In dn̄io .ē una car̄. 7 X. uilti 7 II . borđ cū . II .car̄ 7 dimiđ.

Ibi . X . ac̄ pti. Silua . I. leuū lḡ. 7 V . q̄rent̷ lat.

Valuit. X. ſoī. Modo. C.X. ſoliđ.

IN WICESLE HĐ.

Ipſa æccła ten̄ *TEDINWELLE*. Ibi ſunt. V . hidæ. 7 una v̄ træ.

Tra̷.ē.VIII.car̄. In dn̄io ſunt. II.7 XXIIII. uilti 7 XI. borđ cū. VII.

car̄. Ibi . II . molini de. XXIIII. ſoī 7 XX. ac̄ pti. Valuit. X . ſoī. Modo

VII . liḃ.

EN7   [In WITCHLEY Wapentake]
  2. Walter holds 2 hides in LYDDINGTON from the Bishop himself.
STOKE (Dry), 'SNELSTON' and CALDECOTT belong to it.
Land for 16 ploughs in total. In lordship 6 ploughs; 4 slaves;
    26 villagers and 24 smallholders who have 9 ploughs.
    2 mills at 8s; meadow, 28 acres; woodland 3 furlongs long
      and 2 furlongs wide.
Value of the whole £8.
Bardi held it, with full jurisdiction.

EN8 3 Walter holds 1 hide in ESSENDINE from the Bishop also.
Land for 6 ploughs. In lordship 2, with 1 slave;
    16 villagers and 5 smallholders with 4 ploughs.
    A mill at 16s; meadow, 3 acres; woodland 6 furlongs long and
      4 furlongs wide.
The value was £4; now 100s.
Bardi held it, with full jurisdiction.

6   LAND OF PETERBOROUGH [ABBEY]...   221 b

  10 The Church holds 6 hides itself in OUNDLE. . . . . . .

EN9   In WITCHLEY Hundred
To this manor belong 2 hides and 1 virgate of land in STOKE (?Dry).
Land for 8 ploughs. In lordship 1 plough;
    10 villagers and 2 smallholders with 2½ ploughs.   221 c
    Meadow, 10 acres; woodland 1 league long and
      5 furlongs wide.
The value was 10s; now 110s.
    . . . .
EN10 In WITCHLEY Hundred
  13 The Church holds TINWELL itself. 5 hides and 1 virgate of land.
Land for 8 ploughs. In lordship 2;
    24 villagers and 11 smallholders with 7 ploughs.
    2 mills at 24s; meadow, 20 acres.
The value was 10s; now £7.

XXVI. TERRA ROBERTI DE TODENI.

Idē teñ.1.hiđ 7 unā bouatā trǣ *IN WICESLEA WAPENT.*
in *SEGENTONE.*Tra.ē.IIII.car̄.In dn̄io ſunt.ii.7 ii.
ſerui.7 VIII.uilli 7 II.borđ cū p̄ro hn̄t.1.car̄ 7 dim̄.
Ibi.III.ac̄ p̄ti.Silua.1.q̇ẓ lḡ.7 altera lat̄.Roḃtus
n̄ hr̄ niſi.III.parte ſiluæ.Similit de tra arabili.
Ad hanc trā ptin una v̄ trǣ in *BERCHEDONE.*Ibi ſt̄
IIII.uilli cū dimiđ car̄.
Valuit.XL.ſoł.Modo.XX.ſoł.

.XXX.   TERRA WILLELMI PEVREL.

Wap   *IN WICESLEA HD.*

Sasfrid teñ de.W.II.hiđ 7 dimiđ in *EPINGEHA.*
Tra.ē.IIII.car̄.In dn̄io.ē una.cū.1.ſeruo.7 VIII.uilli
7 IIII.borđ cū.II.car̄.Ibi moliñ 7 dim̄ de.XII.ſoliđ.
7 IIII.ac̄ p̄ti.7 VI.ac̄ ſiluæ.Valuit 7 uał.XX.ſoliđ.ſ HD.
Eduuard 7 Fredgis tenuer̄ cū ſaca 7 ſoca. *IN GRAVESEND*

.XXXV. TERRA WILLI FILIJ ANSCVLF *IN WICESLEA WAP.*

Wills filỻ Anſculfi 7 Roḃt de eo teñ dim̄ hiđ
in *TOLTORP.*Tra.ē.IIII.car̄.Rex inde hr̄ ſocā.
In dn̄io.ē una.7 XII.uilli 7 XV.borđ hn̄t.III.car̄.
Ibi.IIII.molini de.XL.ſoliđ.7 XX.ac̄ p̄ti.VIII.ſochi tenuer̄.
Valuit.XL.ſoł.Modo.c.ſoliđ.

26   LAND OF ROBERT OF TOSNY ...   225 a

EN11 In WITCHLEY Wapentake
  3 He also holds 1 hide and 1 bovate of land in SEATON.
  Land for 4 ploughs. In lordship 2; 2 slaves.
    8 villagers and 2 smallholders with a priest have 1½ ploughs.
    Meadow, 3 acres; woodland 1 furlong long and another wide.
      Robert has only the third part of the woodland; the same
      with the arable land.

  1 virgate of land in BARROWDEN belongs to this land.
    4 villagers there with ½ plough.
  The value was 40s; now 20s.

[35]   LAND OF WILLIAM PEVEREL ...   225 d

                                                  226 a

Wap' In WITCHLEY Hundred
EN12 9 Sasfrid holds 2½ hides from William in EMPINGHAM.
  Land for 4 ploughs. In lordship 1, with 1 slave;
    8 villagers and 4 smallholders with 2 ploughs.
    1½ mills at 12s; meadow, 4 acres; woodland, 6 acres.
  The value was and is 20s.
    Edward and Fredegis held it, with full jurisdiction.

[36]   LAND OF WILLIAM SON OF ANSCULF

EN13 In WITCHLEY Wapentake
  1 William son of Ansculf holds ½ hide in TOLETHORPE, and   226 b
  Robert from him. Land for 4 ploughs. The King has the
  jurisdiction from it. In lordship 1 (plough).
    12 villagers and 15 smallholders have 3 ploughs.
    4 mills at 40s; meadow, 20 acres.
    8 Freemen held it.
  The value was 40s; now 100s.

XLVI. TERRA GISLEBTI DE GAND.

Ipſe . Gi . teñ EPINGEHĀ Ibi ſt . IIII . hidæ. De his . III . in dñio.
Tra . ē . VIII . cař. In dñio ſt . IIII . cař . 7 VIII . ſerui . 7 xv . uilti
cū . IIII . cař . Ibi . v . molini de . XLII . ſol 7 VIII . deñ . 7 x . ac̄
p̄ti . Silua . I . q̄ʒ lḡ . 7 x . p̄tic lat̄ . Valuit . c . ſol . M̈ . x . liɓ.
Ipſe teñ in ead uilla . VII . hiđ 7 dimiđ 7 unā bouatā træ
de ſoca regis de Roteland . 7 dicit regē ſuū aduocat̄ eſſe.
Tra . ē . xv . cař . Has hñt ibi . XIIII . ſochi cū . L . 7 uno uilto.
Ibi . v . molini de . XXIIII . ſol . 7 x . ac̄ p̄ti . 7 x . ac̄ ſiluæ.
Valuit 7 ual . VIII . liɓ.

.LVI. TERRA JVDITÆ COMITISSÆ. IN WICELEA WAPENT.

JVDITA Comitiſſa teñ de rege . I . hiđ 7 dim̄ in RIEHALE.
Tra . ē . VIII . cař cū appendic̄ . In dñio . ē una . 7 IIII . ſerui . 7 x.
uilti 7 IIII . ſochi hñt . IIII . cař . Ibi . II . molini de . XXXVI . ſolid.
Silua . IIII . q̄rent lḡ . 7 II . q̄ʒ lat̄.
Huic ⊕ p̄tiñ BELMESTORP . Ibi . I . hida 7 dimiđ . 7 in dñio . II.
cař . 7 XIIII . uilti 7 VI . borđ hñt . IIII . cař . Ibi moliñ de . x . ſol.
7 VIII . deñ . 7 XVI . ac̄ p̄ti . Tot̄ ualuit 7 ual . VI . liɓ.

Roɓt teñ de . Co . II . hiđ 7 unā v træ in BITLESBROCH.
Tra . ē . III . cař 7 dim̄ . In dñio . ē una 7 II . ſerui . 7 XII . uilti
cū . IIII . borđ hñt . II . cař 7 dim̄ . Ibi . xx . ac̄ p̄ti . Silua
minuta . I . q̄ʒ 7 dim̄ in lḡ . 7 tntđ in lat̄ . Valuit . xx . ſol.
Modo . xxx . ſolid . Eduuarđ tenuit cū ſaca 7 ſoca.

46   LAND OF GILBERT OF GHENT...   227 c

[In WITCHLEY Wapentake]

EN14 4 Gilbert holds EMPINGHAM himself. 4 hides. 3 of them in lordship.
Land for 8 ploughs. In lordship 4 ploughs; 8 slaves;
    15 villagers with 4 ploughs.
    5 mills at 42s 8d; meadow, 10 acres; woodland 1 furlong
        long and 10 perches wide.
The value was 100s; now £10.

EN15 5 He holds 7½ hides and 1 bovate of land himself
in the same village, of the King's Jurisdiction of Rutland;
he states that the King is his patron. Land for 15 ploughs.
    14 Freemen with 51 villagers have them there.
    5 mills at 24s; meadow, 10 acres; woodland, 10 acres.
The value was and is £8.

56   LAND OF COUNTESS JUDITH   228 b

In WITCHLEY Wapentake

EN16 1 Countess Judith holds 1½ hides from the King in RYHALL.
Land for 8 ploughs, with dependencies. In lordship 1;
4 slaves.
    10 villagers and 4 Freemen have 4 ploughs.
    2 mills at 36s; woodland 4 furlongs long and 2 furlongs wide.

    BELMESTHORPE belongs to this manor. 1½ hides. In lordship 2 ploughs.
    14 villagers and 6 smallholders have 4 ploughs.
    A mill at 10s 8d; meadow, 16 acres.
The value of the whole was and is £6.

....

[In WITCHLEY Wapentake]

EN17 25 Robert holds 2 hides and 1 virgate of land from the Countess   228 c
in BISBROOKE. Land for 3½ ploughs. In lordship 1; 2 slaves.
    12 villagers with 4 smallholders have 2½ ploughs.
    Meadow, 20 acres; underwood 1½ furlongs in length
        and as much in width.
The value was 20s; now 30s.
    Edward held it, with full jurisdiction.

Grimbald teñ de . Co . iii . hiđ una bouata miñ in *TICHECOTE.*
Ťra . ē . vi . cař . In dñio . ē una . 7 viii . ſochi cū . xii . uiłłis 7 uno
borđ hñt . v . cař . Ibi moliñ de . xxiiii . ſoliđ . 7 xii . ac p̃ti .
Valuit . xxx . ſoliđ . Modo . l . ſoliđ . Eduuarđ tenuit . 7 hanc

Iđē teñ de . Co . i . hiđā in *HORNE* . Ťra . ē . ii . cař . In dñio . ē una .
7 ii . ſerui . 7 ii . ancillæ . 7 ix . uiłti cū . iiii . borđ hñt . ii . cař .
Ibi moliñ de . iiii . ſoł 7 viii . deñ . Valuit . xx . ſoł . m̃ . xxx . ſoliđ .

Willelm̃ teñ de . Co . iiii . hiđ in *GLADESTONE* . Ťra . ē
viii . cař . In dñio . ē ; i . cař 7 dim̃ . 7 ii . ſerui . 7 v . uiłti
7 iii . ſochi cū . ii ; borđ hñt . v . cař . Ibi . x . ac p̃ti .
Valuit 7 uał . xl . ſoliđ . Eduuarđ tenuit cū ſaca 7 ſoca .
Huic m̃ ptiñ . vi . ſochi in *LVFENHA* m̃ regis . 7 uñ in
SEGESTONE . 7 uñ in *TORP* . quoℨ pecuñia ſup̃ notata . ē .

.LVIII. TERRA DAVID.

David teñ de rege . iii . v̇ træ in *CASTRETONE* . Ťra . ē . i . cař
7 dimiđ . In dñio tam̃ . ē una cař . 7 vi . uiłti cū p̃bro 7 iii . borđ
hñt . ii . cař . Ibi . ii . ſerui . 7 moliñ de . xii . ſoł . 7 v . ac p̃ti .
Valet . xl . ſoł . Oſgot tenuit cū ſaca 7 ſoca .

EN18 26 Grimbald holds 3 hides, less 1 bovate, from the Countess in
TICKENCOTE. Land for 6 ploughs. In lordship 1.
    8 Freemen with 12 villagers and 1 smallholder have 5 ploughs.
    A mill at 24s; meadow, 12 acres.
The value was 30s; now 50s.
    Edward held it also.

EN19 27 He also holds 1 hide from the Countess in HORN. Land for 2
ploughs. In lordship 1; 2 male and 2 female slaves.
    9 villagers with 4 smallholders have 2 ploughs.
    A mill at 4s 8d.
The value was 20s; now 30s.
....

[In WITCHLEY Wapentake]
EN20 36 William holds 4 hides from the Countess in GLASTON.   228 d
Land for 8 ploughs. In lordship 1½ ploughs; 2 slaves.
    5 villagers and 3 Freemen with 2 smallholders have 5 ploughs.
    Meadow, 10 acres.
The value was and is 40s.
    Edward held it, with full jurisdiction.

To this manor belong 6 Freemen in LUFFENHAM, the King's
manor, 1 in SEATON, and 1 in THORPE (by Water), whose
resources are noted above.

<h2>58   LAND OF DAVID   229 b</h2>

[In WITCHLEY Wapentake]
EN21 1 David holds 3 virgates of land from the King in CASTERTON.
Land for 1½ ploughs. In lordship, however, 1 plough.
    6 villagers with a priest and 3 smallholders have 2 ploughs.
    2 slaves; a mill at 12s; meadow, 5 acres.
Value 40s.
    Osgot held it, with full jurisdiction.

STANFORD BVRGV REGIS . dedit geldũ T.R.E.

pro . XII . hundrez 7 dimidio . In exercitu . 7 naui

gio . 7 in Danegeld . Ibi fuer 7 funt . VI . cuftodię.

Quinq, in Lincolefcỹre . 7 fexta in Hantunefcỹre . quæ

eſt ultra pontẽ . 7 tã ipſa reddebat omẽ cſuetudinẽ

cũ alijs . pter gablũ 7 theloneũ . qđ abb de Burg

habebat 7 habet.

Edded regina hb . LXX . maũs quæ jacuer in Roteland

cũ oĩibz cſuetudinibz . fine panificis . Ad has adjaceɴ

II . car træ 7 dimiđ . 7 I . caruca araɴs . 7 XLV . ac pti ext uillã,

Modo hr Rex . W . 7 ualet VI . lib . T.R.E.ual . IIII . lib.

Albt unã æcctam S Petri cũ . II . maũs . 7 dim car tre quæ

jacet in Rotelande in hemeldune . Val . x . foliđ.

.XIII.   TERRA HVGONIS COMITIS.

SVD REDING

In *EXEWELLE* . hb Harold . II . car træ ad gld . Tra ad . VI.

car . Ibi Gozelin hõ comit . H . hr . II . car . 7 XIII . uilt . 7 II.

borđ . hñtes . v . car . 7 XVI . ac pti . T.R.E. ual . c . foliđ.

m . VI . lib.

.XXIIII.   TERRA GISLEBERTI DE GAND.

In *BVRGELAI* . hb Vlf . II . car tre ad gld . Tra . VII . car.

Ibi hr Goisfriđ hõ Gislebti . II . car . 7 XXX . uilt . 7 VII.

borđ . cũ . IIII . car . 7 XXX . ac pti . Siluæ . I . lev lg . 7 III . q̃z

lat . T.R.E. ual . IIII . lib . m c . fot.

S   STAMFORD, the King's Borough   336 d
ELc1 1   gave tax before 1066 for 12½ Hundreds; for the army, in
ship service, and in Danegeld. There were and are six wards,
five in Lincolnshire, the sixth in Northamptonshire; it is across
the bridge; however, it paid all customary dues with the others,
except tribute and tolls, which the Abbot of Peterborough
had and has.

....

ELc2 9   Queen Edith had 70 residences which lay in Rutland,
with all customary dues except the bakers'. Attached to
them are 2½ carucates of land and 1 plough, which is
ploughing, and 45 acres of meadow outside the town.
King William has them now.
Value £6; value before 1066 £4.

....

ELc3 13   Albert (has) 1 church, St. Peter's, with 2 residences and ½
carucate of land, which lies in Rutland, in Hambleton.
Value 10s.

13   **LAND OF EARL HUGH**   349 a

SOUTH RIDING ...   349 c

ELc4 8 In ASHWELL   Earl Harold had 2 carucates of land taxable. Land   349 d
M.   for 6 ploughs. Jocelyn, Earl H(ugh)'s man, has 2 ploughs and
13 villagers and 2 smallholders who have 5 ploughs.
Meadow, 16 acres.
Value before 1066, 100s; now £6.   *(R 16)*

24   **LAND OF GILBERT OF GHENT ...**   354 c

ELc5 78 In BURLEY   Ulf had 2 carucates of land taxable.   355 d
M.   Land for 7 ploughs. Geoffrey, Gilbert's man, has 2 ploughs and
30 villagers and 7 smallholders with 4 ploughs.
Meadow, 30 acres; woodland, 1 league long and
3 furlongs wide.
Value before 1066 £4; now 100s.   *(R 15)*

.XXVI.   TERRA ALVREDI DE LINCOLE.

ᛘ In *WIME* ħƀ Siuuard . IIII . caȓ træ ad glđ . Tra . IIII . caȓ.

Ibi Gleu hō Aluredi hȓ . I . caȓ . 7 XI . uiłł 7 III . borđ.

cū . III . caȓ . 7 c . acs p̄ti . VI . min . 7 q̄t XX . acs filuæ past.

T.R.E. uał XL. foł. m̂ . L . Tailla . X . fol. H̄ SOCA . ē in Tiftel

ᛘ In *TISTELTVNE* . ħƀ Siuuard dim̄ caȓ tre   ƒtune.

ad glđ . Tra . I . caȓ . Ibi Gleu hō Alurđ hȓ . I . caȓ . 7 III .

uiłł 7 II . borđ cū đ . caȓ . p̄ciū ej in Wime.   SOCA

ᛋ In alia Tifteltune . I . caȓ træ ad glđ . Tra . I . caȓ . Ibi . II .

foċħ hn̄t III . boū in caȓ.

.LI.   TERRA GODEFRIDI DE CAMBRAI.

In *TISTELTVNE* ħƀ Turuert, . I . caȓ 7 dim̄ ƒ Warnode.

ad glđ . Tra . XII . boū . Ibi Gleu hō Godef hȓ . I . foċħ

7 III . borđ cū dim̄ caȓ . 7 XV . acs filuæ . 7 XL . acs in War

node Drogonis . T.R.E. uał . XX . fol . m̂ . X.

[? In BELTISLOE Wapentake]

ELc6 46 In WITHAM Siward had 4 carucates of land taxable.   358 c
M. Land for 4 ploughs. Gleu, Alfred's man, has 1 plough and
11 villagers and 3 smallholders with 3 ploughs.
Meadow, 100 acres, less 6; woodland pasture, 80 acres.
Value before 1066, 40s; now 50[s]; exactions, 10s.
Jurisdiction in Thistleton.

ELc7 47 In THISTLETON Siward had ½ carucate of land taxable.
M. Land for 1 plough. Gleu, Alfred's man, has 1 plough and
3 villagers and 2 smallholders with ½ plough.
Its assessment is in Witham.   JURISDICTION   *(R 9)*

ELc8 48 In another THISTLETON 1 carucate of land taxable.
S. Land for 1 plough.
2 Freemen have 3 oxen in a plough.

ELc9 10 In THISTLETON Thorfreth had 1½ carucates taxable.
Land for 12 oxen. Gleu, Godfrey's man, has
1 Freeman and 3 smallholders with ½ plough.
Woodland, 15 acres; 40 acres in Drogo's *Warnode*.
Value before 1066, 20s; now 10[s].

.LVI. TERRA JVDITÆ COMITISSÆ.

In Offintone.ħƀ Leuric abƀ S̄ Petri de burg .LX .ačs tre fine glđ. Judita comitiffa hanc trā hī.In ea nil pecunie hī.fed colit eā in belmeſtorp ꝳ.

Ϝ Valet .x .ſoł.

ꝳ In OVERTVNE 7 Stratone.ħƀ Waltef comes .III. car tre 7 dim̄ ad glđ .Tra.XII.caꝛ .Ibi Judita comit̄ hī.III.car in dn̄io.7 XXX.V.uiłł.7 VIII.bord.cū.IX.caꝛ.

367 a

7 XL .ačs p̄ti.7 Siluæ paſtił.I.leu lḡ.7 dim̄ lai. T.R.E.uał.x̄ .liƀ.M.̷ XL.liƀ.

ꝳ In TISTERTVNE.ħƀ Erich dim̄ car tre ad glđ .Tra .I.caꝛ.Ibi hī Hugo hō com̄.I.caꝛ.7 VI.uiłł cū.I.caꝛ. T.R.E.uał.xx .ſoł.m̄.XL.

ꝳ In WICHINGEDENE.ħƀ Wallef.IIII.caꝛ træ ad glđ. Tra.XII.caꝛ.Ibi Hugo hō comitiffæ hī.V.car in dn̄io. 7 XXVII.uiłł 7 VII.bord.cū.VIII.caꝛ.Pratū.x.q̂ƺ lḡ.7 VIII.q̂ƺ lai.

[In NESS Wapentake]

ELc10 4 In UFFINGTON Abbot Leofric of Peterborough had 60 acres
of land without tax. ..... Countess Judith has this land.
She has no livestock on it, but cultivates in the
manor of Belmesthorpe.
Value 10s.

....

ELc11 11 In (Market) OVERTON and STRETTON Earl Waltheof
M. had 3½ carucates of land taxable. Land for 12 ploughs.
Countess Judith has 3 ploughs in lordship and
35 villagers and 8 smallholders with 9 ploughs.
Meadow, 40 acres; woodland pasture 1 league long   367 a
and ½ wide.
Value before 1066 £12; now £40.   (R 7)

ELc12 12 In THISTLETON Eric had ½ carucate of land taxable.
M. Land for 1 plough. Hugh, the Countess' man, has
1 plough and
6 villagers with 1 plough.
Value before 1066, 20s; now 40[s].   (R 8)

ELc13 13 In WHISSENDINE Earl Waltheof had 4 carucates of land taxable.
M. Land for 12 ploughs. Hugh, the Countess' man,
has 5 ploughs in lordship and
27 villagers and 7 smallholders with 8 ploughs.
Meadow, 10 furlongs long and 8 furlongs wide.
[Value.......]   (R 11)

....

Ⓜ In EXENTVNE . ħɓ Wallef^{com} . II . caŕ trǽ ad glđ . Tŕa
XII . car̄ . Ibi ħt Juđ comit . III . car̄ . 7 XXX.VII . uiłt .
cū . VIII . car̄ . 7 II . moliñ . XIII . folid . ptū . VI . q̃ʒ lḡ.
Silua paſt p̱ loca . V . q̃ʒ lḡ . 7 V . lat̄ . T.R.E . uał . VIII . liɓ

{ Similit
In Rote
lande

Ⓜ In WITEWELLE ħɓ Befy . I . caŕ trǽ ad glđ . ſm̄ . X . liɓ
Tŕa . III . car̄ . Ibi Herbt ħo comit ħt . I . car̄ . 7 VI . uiłt
7 IIII . borđ cū . II . car̄ . Ibi ǽccła 7 pɓr . 7 I . moliñ . XII .
denar . 7 XX . ac̄ p̄ti . Silua paſt . VI . q̃ʒ 7 VI . ptic lḡ.
7 III . q̃ʒ 7 XIII . ptic lat̄ . Vał . XL . fol.

Ⓜ In COLEBY . ħɓ Archil . V . caŕ trǽ ad glđ . Tŕa . V . car̄.
Ibi ħt Juđ comit . I . car̄ . 7 I . focħ de . I . car̄ huj trǽ .
7 VI . uiłt cū . I . car̄ . 7 XXX . ac̄s p̄ti . T.R.E . uał . LX . fol . m̄ . XL .

Ṣ In Wimme . II . caŕ trǽ ad glđ . Tŕa . II . car̄ . Soca in Oure
tone . Ibi . VIII . focħ 7 II . uiłt|ħn̄t . III . car̄ . Ibi dim̄ ǽcła
                ^{7 I.borđ.}
7 LX . ac̄ p̄ti . 7 c . ac̄ filuǽ .
Ṣ In Tifteltone . VI . bou trǽ ad glđ . Tŕa VI . boɓ . Soca ejđ . Ⓜ.
Ibi . II . borđ ħn̄t . II . bou in car̄ . Valet X . fol . Hugo teñ .
Ɓ In Bichere . I . bou tre 7 dim̄ ad glđ . Tŕa . II . bou . Inland
in Wime . Wafta . ē p̄ter unā falinā .

In RUTLAND

Lc14 17 In EXTON Earl Waltheof had 2 carucates of land taxable.

M. Land for 12 ploughs. Countess Judith has 3 ploughs and
37 villagers with 8 ploughs.
2 mills, 13s; meadow 6 furlongs long; woodland,
pasture in places, 5 furlongs long and 5 wide.
Value before 1066 £8; now £10.   *(R 12)*

Likewise in RUTLAND

Lc15 18 In WHITWELL Besi had 1 carucate of land taxable.

M. Land for 3 ploughs. Herbert, the Countess' man, has 1 plough and
6 villagers and 4 smallholders with 2 ploughs.
A church and a priest; 1 mill, 12d; meadow, 20 acres;
woodland pasture 6 furlongs and 6 perches long
and 3 furlongs and 13 perches wide.
Value 40s.   *(R 13)*

Lc16 19 In COLEBY Arkell had 5 carucates of land taxable.

M. Land for 5 ploughs. Countess Judith has 1 plough and
1 Freeman with 1 carucate of this land,
and 6 villagers with 1 plough.
Meadow, 30 acres.
Value before 1066, 60s; now 40[s].

20 In WITHAM 2 carucates of land taxable.

S. Land for 2 ploughs. Jurisdiction in (Market) Overton.
8 Freemen, 2 villagers and 1 smallholder have 3 ploughs.
Half a church; meadow, 60 acres; woodland, 100 acres.

Lc17 21 In THISTLETON 6 bovates of land taxable. Land for 6 oxen.

S. Jurisdiction of this manor.
2 smallholders have 2 oxen in a plough.
Value 10s.
Hugh holds it.

22 In BICKER 1½ bovates of land taxable. Land for 2 oxen.

B. *Inland* in Witham. Waste, apart from 1 salt-house.

CLAMORES IN CHETSTEVEN.

Sexaginta acs̃ trǣ quas Iudita comitiſſa h̃t 7 colit
cū carucis de belmeſtorp . dicit Wapent̃ q̃d S̃ Petrus de
burg habuit . T.R.E.
De his . LX acris tr̃e 7 de . XLVIII . acris p̃ti:́ iacet War
node in Offintone Aluredi de Lincolia . ſed ui eſt retenta.

Archieps̄ Ældred᷎ adq̃ſiuit Lauintone 7 Schillintone
cū BEREW᷎ Harduic . de Vlf tope ſune . p̃ pecuniā ſuā
quā ei dedit uidente Wapent̃ .7 poſtea uider̃ ſigillū
regis p̃ q̃d reſaiſit᷎ eſt de ipſis terris . quia Hilbold᷎ eū
diſſaiſierat de eis.

TERRA REGIS.

In NOSSITONE s̃t . III . car̃ trǣ p̃tin̄ ad ſocā de OCHEHA.̃
Ibi . XVII . ſochi cū . VI . bord h̃nt . VI . car̃ .7 ibi . I . q̃ꝫ ſiluæ
in lḡ .7 dim q̃ꝫ lat̃ . Valet . XX . ſolid̃ . Rex h̃t in dñio.

ELc18 2 The Wapentake states that before 1066 (the Abbot of)
Peterborough had 60 acres of land which Countess Judith
has (in UFFINGTON) and cultivates with the Belmesthorpe
ploughs. Of these 60 acres of land, and of 48 acres of meadow,
the *Warnode* lies in (the lands of) Alfred of Lincoln's Uffington,
but has been withheld by force.   *(ELc 10)*

....

ELc19 10 Archbishop Aldred acquired LAVINGTON and SKILLINGTON, with
the outlier, HARDWICK, from Ulf, Topi's son, with his own money,
which he gave him in the sight of the Wapentake; and later they
saw the King's seal, through which he was repossessed of these
lands, because Ilbold had dispossessed him of them.

ELe   LEICESTERSHIRE

[1]   LAND OF THE KING...   230 b

ELe1 11 In KNOSSINGTON 3 carucates of land, which belong to   230 d
the jurisdiction of Oakham.
17 Freemen with 6 smallholders have 6 ploughs.
Woodland, 1 furlong in length and ½ furlong wide.
Value 20s.
The King has it in lordship.

NOTES

ABBREVIATIONS used in the notes.

ASC . . . *The Ango-Saxon Chronicle* (translated G.N. Garmonsway) London 1960
DB . . . Domesday Book. DBL . . . C.W. Foster and T. Longley *The Lincolnshire
Domesday and the Lindsey Survey* (Introduction by F.M. Stenton) Lincs. Record
Society 19 (1924, reprint 1976). Ducange . . . G.A.L. Henschel (ed.) *Glossarium
Mediae et Infimae Latinitatis* Niort and London 1884-7. DG . . . H.C. Darby and
G,R. Versey *Domesday Gazetteer* Cambridge 1975. DGM . . . H.C. Darby and I.B.
Terrett *The Domesday Geography of Midland England* Cambridge 2nd edition
1971 pp. 359-383. Ekwall . . . E. Ekwall *The Concise Oxford Dictionary of
English Place-Names* Oxford 4th edition 1960. Ellis . . . H. Ellis *General Intro-
duction to Domesday Book* folio edition DB 4, i-cvii; quarto edition 1833 (reprint
1971). FA . . . *Inquisitions and Assessments relating to Feudal Aids with other
analogous Documents preserved in the Public Records Office AD 1284-1431*
London 1899-1920 6 vols. FE . . . J.H. Round *Feudal England* London 1895.
Finberg . . . H.P.R. Finberg *Gloucestershire Studies* Leicester 1957. Finn . . .
R. Welldon Finn *An Introduction to Domesday Book* London 1963. Forssner
. . . T. Forssner *Continental-Germanic Personal Names in Old and Middle English
Times* Uppsala 1916. Geld Roll . . . in A.J. Robertson *Anglo-Saxon Charters*
1939 pp. 230-7; 481-4. Hart . . . C. Hart *The Hidation of Northamptonshire*
Leicester 1970 (Department of English Local History, Occasional Papers, Second
Series No. 3). KCD . . . J.M. Kemble *Codex Diplomaticus Aevi Saxonici* London
1839 - 48, 6 vols. LSR . . . R.E. Glasscock (ed.) *The Lay Subsidy of 1334*
London 1975. MS . . . Manuscript. Maitland . . . F.W. Maitland *Domesday Book
and Beyond* Cambridge 1897. Mon. Ang. . . . W. Dugdale *Monasticon Anglicanum*
London 1846, 6 vols. ODan . . . Old Danish. OE . . . Old English OEB . . .
G. Tengvik *Old English Bynames* Uppsala 1938 (Nomina Germanica 4). OFr . . .
Old French. OG . . . Old German. OHG . . . Old High German. ON . . . Old
Norse. PNDB . . . O. von Feilitzen *The Pre-Conquest Personal Names of Domes-
day Book* Uppsala 1937 (Nomina Germanica 3). Reg . . . *Regesta Regum Anglo-
Normannorum 1066-1154* (ed. H.W.C. Davis, C. Johnson, H.A. Cronne) Oxford
1913 on. RH . . . *Rotuli Hundredorum* Record Commission 1812 -18, 2 vols.
RMLWL . . . R.E. Latham *Revised Medieval Latin Wordlist* London 1965.
Survey . . . 12th Century Survey of Northamptonshire in VCH Northants. i pp. 357-
389. VCH . . . Victoria County History (Rutland vol i (1908)).

The editor is grateful to Mr. J.D. Foy for reading the proofs.

The later county of Rutland was only part-formed at the time of the Domesday
Survey. Of the three Wapentakes which were to comprise the county, only
Martinsley and Alstoe were counted as *Roteland* in 1086. Witchley, the third,
though north of the river Welland, was an integral part of Northamptonshire.
Entries for it are found scattered in the different chapters of tenants-in-chief,
like those of any other hundred, and, like Northamptonshire itself, it is measured
predominantly in hides and virgates, the only area north of the Welland to be
hidated.
     Alstoe and Martinsley, the Domesday *Roteland*, were also anomalous. Their
tenants-in-chief are given on the page of Nottinghamshire landholders, under the
heading *Roteland* (col. 280d), and the three columns of the County's schedule are
an appendix to Nottinghamshire (cols. 293c-294a). Alstoe, divided into two
"hundreds", was attached to two Nottinghamshire Wapentakes, and both Alstoe
and Martinsley were regarded as part of Nottinghamshire for tax purposes (R3).

Roteland was also closely tied to Lincolnshire. Stamford in Ness Wapentake, pinched between Witchley and Northamptonshire proper, had a number of residences in *Roteland* (ELc 2), while itself containing outlying dependencies of Hambleton (R21. ELc 3). Moreover, of the twelve lands in Alstoe, eight are duplicated in the Lincs. folios. They are tabulated at the end of the notes.

Rutland is the only midland shire not to be named after a chief town. The place-name Rutland is explained in Ekwall as 'Rota's Land' from an OE Pers. name *Rota*. But an equally likely origin would be an OE *rote-land* from OE *rot* adj., 'cheerful, pleasant', hence 'the pleasant district, the merry land'; compare *Mondrem* the name of a medieval forest in Cheshire, from the OE *man-dream* 'happiness', and, of course, the numerous 'Beaulieu' names. Like other midland shires, it had been part of Mercia, and was then subject to Danish invasion and occupation.

The county organisation of the midlands probably dates from no earlier than the beginning of the eleventh century, and the counties emerge from areas occupied by individual Danish armies (Finberg 17ff.).

Roteland may at first have been a part of Northants. over the Welland, as Witchley still was in 1086. Overton, Stretton, Whissendine and Exton in Alstoe together with Ryhall and Belmesthorpe in Witchley belonged to Earl Waltheof in 1066 and would most naturally have been administered as part of his Northamptonshire earldom.

The first Wapentake to be detached, thus forming the nucleus of the future county, was probably Martinsley. *Roteland* had been a grant to Emma, mother of Edward the Confessor, on her marriage to Ethelred II in 1002 (Geoffrey Gaimer, *Estorie des Engles* Rolls Series, line 4139). It may previously have been held by Aelfthryth mother of Ethelred, if she is the *Elstruet* of Geoffrey's next line: *ke Elstruet aveit eu devant*. *Roteland* is subsequently held by Queen Edith, wife of the Confessor, (as well as Barrowden and Ketton in Witchley), as evidenced by DB (R 17;19-20) and was probably still hers at her death in 1076. Edward had in fact granted this *Roteland* (clearly only Martinsley Wapentake) to Westminster Abbey (Mon. Ang. i 299 = KCD iv 863) giving Edith only a life interest in the land. The Conqueror usually honoured such grants, but he seems to have retained Martinsley for himself after Edith's death, and was holding it in 1086, though an echo of Westminster's claims are found in the term *Cherchesoch* which describes Oakham, Hambleton and Ridlington in the text (R 17; 19-20 and note). The churches of Martinsley were granted by the Conqueror and confirmed by Rufus to Westminster (Mon. Ang. i 301-2), but Martinsley itself was kept and administered as a soke for successive queens of England.

It is not clear how Martinsley came to be attached to Nottingham. The writ of Edward granting *Roteland* to his queen and to St. Peter's of Westminster is addressed to the sheriff and thanes of Northamptonshire, but the later grant of the churches is sent to Remigius, Bishop of Lincoln, Hugh of Port and all the King's servants (*ministri*) in Nottingham. When Martinsley, probably administered directly for the King by a reeve, was detached from Witchley, Alstoe would have been isolated from Northamptonshire. It was clearly in an especially strange position in 1086. The ploughland totals of Thurgarton and Broxtow Wapentakes in Nottingham are incomplete without additions from the two halves of Alstoe, but the duplicate entries show that it was also considered as part of Lincs. The discrepancies between the duplicate entries for each village suggest that it may have been surveyed twice, once from Notts. and once from Lincs.

After 1086, Rutland gradually evolved into a full county. Witchley is no longer counted as part of Northants. in the 12th century Survey of that County. Under John it is referred to for the first time as a county (*comitatus*) and by the time of the earliest Feudal Aids, at the end of the thirteenth century, it is independent (VCH 167ff.). Oakham later became detached from Martinsley, forming its own soke, and Witchley was divided into two hundreds (EN note).

Alstoe and Martinsley are measured in carucates and bovates, as are Lincs., Notts., Leics., Derbys. and Yorks. The 24 carucates of Alstoe, in two 'hundreds', and the 12 of Martinsley are clear signs of the Danish duodecimal system of measurement, contrasting with the hidation in fives and tens in the south of England. The carucation of DB is clearly not geographical but fiscal. Martinsley, which is roughly the same size as Alstoe, has half the number of carucates, probably because its three royal manors are beneficially assessed. Ploughlands similarly seem to be conventional figures dating from an earlier system of assessment. Alstoe, for example, has 48 lands but 84 actual ploughs. The implication is that *Roteland* had had its assessment reduced, like the rest of Northants., probably as a result of the ravage inflicted by Morcar's army in 1065 (ASC 190-2). On this see VCH Rutland 122 ff., Round in VCH Northants. pp. 258-269, DGM 368, Hart *passim*, John Morris in DB Sussex Appendix and the notes to the Northants. volume in this series.

There is no English Place-Name Society volume for Rutland, but in such a small County identification of places is not difficult. In Witchley Wapentake DB *Lufenhā* and *Castretone* are now represented by North and South Luffenham and Great and Little Casterton, but there is no evidence of the existence of separate villages there in 1086. In these cases, only the larger has been indexed and mapped. In Alstoe, the Lincs. folios refer to Thistleton and 'another' *(alia)* Thistleton, but two villages are not found there in later times. As at Courteenhall (Northants. 35,24) and Seaborough (Somerset 3,1) and elsewhere, *alia* probably refers not to adjacent villages of the same name, but to different holdings in the same village, in this case over the Lincs. border.

The manuscript is written on leaves, or folios, of parchment (sheepskin), measuring about 15in. by 11in. (38 by 28 cm). on both sides. On each side, or page, are two columns, making four to each folio. The folios were numbered in the 17th century and the four columns of each are here lettered a,b,c,d. The manuscript emphasises words and usually distinguishes chapters and sections by the use of red ink. Underlining here indicates deletion.

In other counties, the text of DB is arranged by fiefs with places geographically in the same hundred, dispersed. In Rutland, arrangement is, exceptionally, by hundred in the order Alstoe (northern), Alstoe (southern), Martinsley, with the same tenants-in-chief sometimes occurring more than once. The scribe has made an attempt in the MS to relate these names to the list of Landholders of col. 280d, by means of marginal figures, but these are sporadic and inconsistent. They have been reproduced in the translation, but for the purpose of reference are ignored, the individual sections being numbered consecutively from 1 to 21.

The standard translation of Rutland is by Sir Frank Stenton (VCH). It contains a useful introduction. His identifications of places are adopted by the Domesday Gazetteer. There is a helpful survey of the County in DGM with a brief bibliography.

Rutland was amalgamated with Leicestershire on 1st April 1974.

LANDHOLDERS. Entered at the end of Nottingham Landholders on col. 280d. The whole page is given in the Nottinghamshire volume in this series.

L2   COUNTESS JUDITH. Daughter of King William's half-sister Adelaide and of Lambert, Count of Lens. Widow and heiress of Earl Waltheof.

L3   ROBERT MALET. Lord of the Honour of Graville-Sainte-Honorine in Normandy. Sheriff of Suffolk.

L4   OGER. Elsewhere styled 'the Breton' *(Brito)*. The head of his fief was at Bourne in Lincs. See R 14 note.

L5   GILBERT OF GHENT. Son of Baldwin, Earl of Flanders, whose sister was wife of William the Conqueror.

L6   EARL HUGH. Hugh of Avranches. Earl of Chester (1070-1101), and nephew of King William.

L7   **ALBERT THE CLERK.** Albert of Lorraine, the King's chaplain. See R 21 note.

RUTLAND. *ROTELAND* in red across the top of the page, centred over the two columns 293c and d. There is no heading on 294a.

R1   **WAPENTAKE.** The equivalent of the Hundred in Danish areas.

TWO HUNDREDS. Not named here nor elsewhere, although Teigh (R 10) is said to be 'in the same Hundred'. The places in R5-10 and R11-16 fall into geographically coherent groups and since Countess Judith appears in both, it is apparent that the lands are listed in Hundred groups rather than by fief. Alstoe is not found divided in later documents; its Hundreds are named Northern and Southern for convenience here.

These small hundreds, consisting of 12 carucates, are explained in the Lindsey Survey of c.1115 and are found also in Notts., Leics. and adjacent shires. See DB Notts. S 1, Leics. 1,1a notes and Round FE 73,79.

12 CARUCATES ... 24 PLOUGHS POSSIBLE. The carucate is a measure of land used in Danish districts and presenting the same problems of definition as the hide. See EN1 note; Ellis i, 149; Round FE 35ff.; John Morris in DB Sussex Appendix.

The 12 Carucates in the Northern Hundred (with Ploughlands and Ploughs tabulated as well) seem to be:

	Carucates	Ploughlands	Ploughs
R 5 Greetham	3	8	10
R 6 Cottesmore	3	12	24
R 7 Overton/Stretton	3½	12	12
R 8 Thistleton	½	1	2
R 9 Thistleton	½	1	1½
R10 Teigh	1½	5	6
	12	39	55½

Not counted are the 3¼ carucates included in the Lincs. entries for Thistleton (ELc 8-9;17) which were either omitted from this total, or more likely counted in Lincs, where the lands may also have lain.

The 12 carucates in the Southern Hundred are accounted for by:

	Carucates	Ploughlands	Ploughs
R11 Whissendine	4	12	13
R12 Exton	2	12	11
R13 Whitwell	1	3	3
R14 'Awsthorp'	1	5	6
R15 Burley	2	7	6
R16 Ashwell	2	6	7
	12	45	46

The ploughlands are clearly fiscal assessments, differing from and less than the number of ploughs on the land. VCH 122ff and DGM 370 divide the two Hundreds differently in order to obtain 42 ploughlands in each.

THURGARTON ... BROXTOW. Wapentakes of Notts. with which Alstoe has no geographical connection. Thurgarton contained about 78 carucates and Broxtow about 84. The addition of 12 from each Alstoe Hundred would produce a figure closer to the expected 96. See VCH 126-7.

	Carucates	Ploughlands	Ploughs	
			King	Other
R17 Oakham	4	16	2	37
R19 Hambleton	4	16	5	40
R20 Ridlington	4	16	4	32
	12	48	11	109

R 2 **12 CARUCATES ... 48 PLOUGHS POSSIBLE.** The 12 carucates are accounted for by:

The one carucate held by Leofnoth at Oakham was possibly additional to the four there (R18). Again the ploughlands are nominal, contrasting with 120 ploughs on the land.

THREE LORDSHIP MANORS. Oakham, Hambleton, Ridlington.

14 PLOUGHS CAN PLOUGH. The ploughs in Lordship total 11, with another four possible at Oakham (R17).

R 4 **BLANCHED.** Or Dealbated; *albas, candidas* or *blancas* in DB. A sample of coin was melted to test for the presence of alloy or baser metal. Money could also be said to be blanched when a standard deduction had been made from its face value to allow for clipping or alloying, without a test by fire. See *Dialogus de Scaccario* ed. Johnson (1950) p. 125.

R 5 **MARGINAL I** denotes the King's Land, referring to the List of Landholders col. 280d.

WOODLAND, PASTURE IN PLACES. *silva per loca pastilis*, sometimes (e.g. at Exton ELc 14) *silva pastilis per loca*, literally 'woodland, grazeable in places'. In some of the corresponding Lincs. entries *per loca* is omitted. The extents given in each case suggest compact woodland, the pasture being scattered within it.

VALUE. *Valet, valebat,* normally means the sums due to lords from their lands.

R 6 **MEADOW, 40 ACRES.** The Latin *ibi* ('there', omitted in translation) has been written over the sign for *et* (7) in the MS.

1 LEAGUE. Generally reckoned as a mile and a half, though the term may well have been used loosely in DB. See Round in VCH Northants. p.280.

VALUE 20s. Old English currency lasted for a thousand years until 1971. The pound contained 20 shillings, each of 12 pence, abbreviated £(ibrae), s(olidi), d(enarii). DB often expresses smaller sums above a shilling in pence (e.g. 32d instead of 2s 8d), and sums above a pound in shillings (e.g. 40s in R8).

R 7 **(MARKET) OVERTON.** Market, probably to distinguish it from Cold Overton, just over the border in Leicester.

EARL WALTHEOF. Son of Siward, husband of Countess Judith. Earl of Hunts. and Northants. from 1065, of Northumberland from 1072. Plotted with Earls Ralph and Roger in 1075. Beheaded 1077.

ALFRED OF LINCOLN CLAIMS. Probably adjacent to his holding at Thistleton, R9.

R 9   MARGINAL III. This seems intended to mark a new Landholder,
       although Alfred does not appear in the list at col. 280d. Thistleton
       is among Alfred's lands in the corresponding Lincs. entry (ELc 7),
       where the holder is Gleu, Alfred's man.

       VALUE ... NOW 60s. In the Lincs. entry, the assessment is said to be in
       Witham, but the value of Witham itself is only 50s (ELc 6).

R10   MARGINAL IIII. In error, Robert being the third in the List of Land-
       holders, col. 280d. The mistake is caused by the insertion of a III against
       R9 above.

       IN THE SAME HUNDRED. See R 1 note.

       TEIGH. The place name is interlined.

       GODWIN. Robert Malet's predecessor in Lincs. also.

       4 PLOUGHS. *ii* has been written above the original *ii* in the text.

R11   IN THE MS the figure *ii* is inserted above the *M* ('Manor') probably
       referring to Whissendine as a double manor, as elsewhere in DB (e.g.
       Derbys. 6,94. 13,2). The figure is absent from the Lincs. duplicate entry.
       Countess Judith is number two in the list of Landholders.

       HUGH OF HOTOT. OEB 93.

R13   BESI. PNDB 201.

       6 PERCHES. DB *perca* or *pertica*, a measure of length, generally
       reckoned at 16½ feet, with 40 to the furlong, though a 20 ft perch was
       in use for woodland until the last century. See Ellis i, 158.

       VALUE 20s. An *l* has been superimposed on the second *x* in the MS, though
       Farley reproduces the figure as *xl*. Had the 1066 and 1086 values been the
       same, the formula would have been *valuit et valet xl solidos*, or a variant.
       The correction probably derives from the corresponding Lincs. entry which
       has simply 'value 40s.'

R14   'AWSTHORP'. Midway between Cottesmore and Burley on Speed's
       map of 1610. The land is found as *Alestorp*, held of the fee of Baldwin
       Wake by the Abbot of Bourne in RH ii, 54b; see also Mon. Ang. vi,
       371 and LSR p.247. This suggests that Oger is identical with Oger the
       Breton, Lord of Bourne; see following and L4 note.

       UNGOMAR. Forssner 197 s.v. *Odger* (and n.4), and OEB 202 (where *Oger*
       is erroneously named *Radulf*), both follow Lindkvist (*Nordische Personen-
       namen in England*, Halle 1910, p.170) in supposing ON *Ungmann-*, *Ungmadhr*,
       miswritten. This prompted by taking *Oger* as ODan *Oddgeir*, *Otger*; but it
       could represent OG *Autger*, *Odger*, and the surname could be OG too, e.g. an
       OHG *Jungemar.

R15   ULF. Probably Ulf Fenman (*Fenisc*), predecessor of Gilbert in other
       counties (e.g. Derbys. 13, 1-2).

R17   OAKHAM. Three carucates in Knossington were a Jurisdiction, see ELe 1.

5 OUTLIERS. Only three places are named in Martinsley, leaving the 19 outliers unidentified. Some of the later parish names such as Wing (see Ekwall) certainly existed before 1086. See DGM 364.

CHURCH JURISDICTION. See Introduction to the notes. Westminster continued to have the avowson and to receive dues in the 13th century. See VCH p.133.

QUEEN EDITH. Wife of Edward the Confessor, daughter of Earl Godwin. Died 1076. She held Barrowden and Ketton in Witchley, also land and residences in Stamford attached to *Roteland* (ELc 2).

A PRIEST AND A CHURCH. Held by Albert the Clerk, see R 21.

4 BOVATES. A measure of land, generally reckoned as an eighth of a carucate.

R18   MALSOR. Latin *mala opera*, OFr *malesoeuvres*. He holds in Northants, and his descendants name Milton Malsor.OEB 349.

5 OXEN IN A PLOUGH. Three were probably borrowed from elsewhere since the usual number is eight; see ELc 8.

R19   HAMBLETON. St. Peter's church in Stamford belonged to it; see R 21 and ELc 3. Among its outliers was no doubt Edith Weston (Grid Reference SK 92 05), preserving the name of the Queen.

3 CHURCHES. See R 21 note.

R20   3 CHURCHES. Probably at Uppingham, Wardley and Belton, all to the south of Ridlington. See Mon. Ang. i 301 (xlii).

R21   THE AFORESAID LAND. Singular, so probably Ridlington.

ALBERT THE CLERK. *Albertus Lotharingius* (of Lorraine) in Mon. Ang. i 301 (xliii) which is a grant (see Introduction) of churches in Rutland to Westminster Abbey, with lands pertaining 'as Albert of Lorraine held them'.

ST. PETER'S STAMFORD. In ELc 3 Albert has the church of St. Peter's Stamford with two residences and ½ carucate of land in Hambleton.

EN   With the exception of Hardwick (ELc 19) an outlier of Skillington, all places in Witchley Wapentake were in Northants.in 1086. They are predominantly hidated, but bovates and carucates are also found, as well as a mixture of both systems. Witchley (as *Hwicceslea*) was considered a part of Northants. in the 'Geld Roll', which probably dates from the early years of the Conqueror's reign, and is there divided into two halves, East and West. By the late thirteenth century, Witchley, now a part of Rutland, was divided into two Hundreds, East and Wrangditch. East contained Ketton, Tinwell, Empingham and places to the east. Wrangditch contained Luffenham, Tixover and places west. There is no evidence in the arrangement of Witchley places in the text of DB that it was regarded as falling into two halves in 1086. In the late thirteenth century, a marginal

Rotel (Roteland) was inserted in the MS of DB Northants. against many of the Witchley entries.

EN1 2 HIDES. The hide was a unit of land measurement, either of productivity, extent, or tax liability. It contained four virgates.
Attempts were made to standardise the hide at 120 acres, but incomplete revision left hides of widely different extent in different areas. See John Morris in DB Sussex Appendix.

24 VILLAGERS. The MS is rubbed here. *Vill'i* in the MS, reproduced by Farley as *vill'*.

EN2 SEATON. MEADOW, 4 ACRES. ii is interlined above ii.

LUFFENHAM. Probably the later South Luffenham, since 'Sculthorp' (EN 3) is part of North Luffenham.

EN3 'SCULTHORP' lay about a quarter of a mile to the south-west of North Luffenham. It is included with the latter in LSR p.247.

HUGH OF PORT. From Port-en-Bessin near Bayeux in Normandy, OEB 108. Sheriff of Hampshire, with Basing as head of his fief.

EN4 EARL MORCAR. The Northumbrians deposed Tosti their earl in 1065 and chose Morcar, son of Algar. He marched south , occupied and devastated Northamptonshire, while through Earl Harold he negotiated his creation as Earl of Northumberland.

HUGH SON OF BALDRIC. Sheriff of Nottinghamshire.

EN5 *PORTLAND* ... BOROUGH. The name of the Borough is not given.
Both Peterborough and Stamford have Churches to St. Peter and to All Saints, but the position of the entry after Casterton suggests a place in Witchley. *Portland* is not found as a name in Stamford, but may not be a place-name at all, being 'land of the Market town' or 'land at, or of, a market' see English Place-Name Society Vol.26 (Elements pt.i) s.v. *port*. The bounds of Stamford field were probably different in 1086, with a detached part of Rutland incorporating some of the town, and another part of the town being in Witchley. See R 21, ELc 1 notes.

EN6 THE BISHOP OF DURHAM. William of St. Carilef, or Calais, 1081-96.

LANGFER. PNDB 308.

WITH FULL JURISDICTION. See Technical Terms and Maitland pp. 80-107.

EN7 THE BISHOP OF LINCOLN. Remigius, consecrated 1067, died 1092.

'SNELSTON'. 1½ miles south-east of Stoke Dry, on Speed's map of 1610. *Snelleston* is found with Caldecott in LSR p.247.

EN9 STOKE (? Dry). The Hundred heading in the text is clear, but Stoke Dry is very remote to be an outlier of Oundle, and there is no trace of a Peterborough holding here later. The men of Peterborough Abbey hold Stoke Doyle, near Oundle, in Northants. 6a,19, and since holdings in chapters 6 and 6a are entered in the same order of Hundreds, with Abbey and Abbey's men often holding halves of the same village, Stoke Doyle is the likely identification.

EN12 WITCHLEY HUNDRED. *Wap'* (for Wapentake) is written in the left margin of the MS.

EN13 WILLIAM SON OF ANSCULF. William of *Pinkeni* (Picquigny). See Wilts. 24, 19. 68,22-23. He was lord of Dudley Castle and an important figure in the midland counties.

EN15 RUTLAND. I.e. in Martinsley or Alstoe Wapentakes. The nearest royal holding to Empingham is Hambleton (R 19).

EN16 4 SLAVES. So MS and Farley; the facsimile, however, has reproduced the dot after the *iiii* as another *i*, thus apparently 5 slaves.

BELMESTHORPE. Judith's ploughs cultivate Uffington (ELc 18).

EN18 ALSO. *et hanc* could refer to the next entry.

EN20 RESOURCES. Elsewhere in DB *pecunia* means 'livestock' or 'goods', (RMLWL. s.v. *pecunia*). Here it seems to replace a value clause. No livestock is mentioned in EN 2 to which this entry refers. DGM p.361 prefers to see this as an example of incomplete revision, since the original returns contained livestock.

ELc   Eight entries, set out in a table at the end, duplicate information for Alstoe, with variation of detail. Hundred heads are inserted conjecturally for Lincs. manors, but not for those in Alstoe, since it is unclear where they were considered to be in 1086 from the point of view of the commissioners surveying Lincs.

ELc1 SHIP SERVICE ... DANEGELD. Taxes levied on Boroughs and shires to pay for the expulsion of the Danish armies.

THE SIXTH IN NORTHAMPTONSHIRE. South of Stamford Bridge, later known as Stamford Baron.

THE ABBOT OF PETERBOROUGH. The ward lay in Upton Hundred, the Abbot of Peterborough's own soke.

ELc2 70 RESIDENCES WHICH LAY IN RUTLAND. *Roteland* proper is separated from Stamford by Witchley Wapentake, but the number of residences, and the mention of meadow outside the town suggest land adjacent to Stamford. Rather than assume that Rutland here means Witchley, it is more likely that a part of Stamford field was in 1086 regarded as a detached part of *Roteland*. See R 21 note.

EXCEPT THE BAKERS'. *'panificis'* is probably the adjective governing *consuetudinibus*, rather than the noun 'baker'. See DBL xxxv and p.7; also J. Tait *The Medieval English Borough*, Manchester (1936), p.109 note.

KING WILLIAM HAS THEM NOW. He retained Edith's lands after her death. See R 17 note.

ELc3 ST. PETER'S. See R 21: 'Albert holds St. Peter's of Stamford which belongs to Hambleton'.

WHICH LIES IN RUTLAND. The *quae* refers to the half carucate. St. Peter's was in Stamford though attached to Hambleton.

ELc6   EXACTIONS. Paid to the Lord. *Tailla* in DB, unlike the later *Tallagium* is normally confined to larger manors with *sochemanni*, especially in North-East Mercia. The word is regularly explained as *exactio*. See texts cited in Ducange s.v. *Tailla* 8 and DB Notts. 9, 74.

ELc7   ASSESSMENT IN WITHAM. This seems to imply that Thistleton is a *soca* (jurisdiction) of Witham, rather than a full manor, despite the marginal M here and in the corresponding R 9 where it has its own value clause. *Soca* is written in the right-hand margin of the MS perhaps to correct the marginal M.

ELc8   ANOTHER THISTLETON. On *alia* see introduction. This part of the village, which has no corresponding Rutland entry, was probably counted as part of Lincs. See R 1 note.

3 OXEN IN A PLOUGH. See R 18 note.

ELc9   GODFREY OF CAMBRAI. Holder of land in Leicestershire.

THORFRETH. DB *Turuert.* ON **Thorfrǿdhr.* See PNDB 392.

DROGO'S WARNODE. In DB the word is found in Lincolnshire of seven places in the south of Kesteven. It is used only of areas of woodland, or meadow, usually of 40 or 60 acres, with one exception, the claim for Uffington (ELc 18). Here the wording seems to include with the 48 acres of meadow, '60 acres of land', held without tax (*sine geldo*), unstocked, but worked from the adjacent manor of Belmesthorpe. The wording varies. On six occasions the acres are '*in Warnode*' of a named landholder; twice the *Warnode* lies in or belongs to (*iacet in* or *pertinet ad*) a particular manor; once the landholder *in silva Westbitham ... habet xl acras pro viii den' Warnode*, and once he withheld *Warnode de x acris prati* in *eadem Beltone.* Here two figures are given, 8d for 40 acres, and 4d for 60 acres, both of woodland. The phrasing suggests a payment made to, or through, a manor or lord. Stenton in DBL (p.xxxviii) noted that in later times the sum was increased if payment was delayed, and describes it as 'rent'. See Ducange s.v. *Warnode* quoting a plea roll of 33 Ed I. Foster in DBL translates (p.29) 'for the purposes of defence against the geld'. Maitland p.123 suggests *War-* (presumably intending 'defence obligation'; from OE *wara*, genitive *ware-* 'defence, watch') and OE suffix *-notu* ('business', 'office'). Finn p.259 links *Warnode* with *wara* ('war') and the better known *warland* which he contrasts with *inland*. An example not cited by Finn is Reg iii 192/3 which mentions two hides near Cirencester (Glos.) in 1152/3, one in Lordship, the other *de warlande quam iiii^{or} villani tenuerunt.* An alternative possibility is an OE **warnodh* 'a warning, an admonition', from OE *war(e)nian* 'to beware, to take heed; to put on guard, to warn; to see to something', see Bosworth-Toller *An Anglo-Saxon Dictionary*; (cf. DB *monere* 'warn', 'summon for military or other duty'). However, since the word is restricted to a small area which had probably once been attached to the maintenance of the Danish borough of Stamford, it may be of Scandinavian origin and could be a usage of the recorded cognates, early Danish *vaerned*, 'assurance, pledge', or the Norwegian-Icelandic *varnadhr*, 'protection, warning, caution'; see Cleasby and Vigfusson *Icelandic-English Dictionary* (2nd edition *ed.* Craigie).

ELc10 ABBOT OF PETERBOROUGH. The land has been alienated from the Church, hence the unusual arrangements for cultivation. See the Claim ELc 18.

LIVESTOCK. See EN 20 note.

BELMESTHORPE. See EN 16.

ELc11 VALUE ... £12. *ii* is interlined above *x* in the MS.

ELc13 [VALUE].The value clause is omitted. See R 11.

ELc15 LIKEWISE IN RUTLAND. Written in the left-hand margin of the MS.

ELc16 COLEBY. Near Boothby Graffoe, (Boothby, or Boby, Wapentake) just south of Lincoln. It is remote from Witham, but is included here as the head manor of which Witham could be a jurisdiction. Witham is however separated from Coleby by a gap in the MS and is attached to Market Overton.

ELc17 THISTLETON. See R 1 note.

JURISDICTION OF THIS MANOR. Presumably of Market Overton.

INLAND. The lord's land, usually exempt from tax; comparable with *dominium* ('Lordship'). See English Place-Names Society Vol.25 (Elements pt.i) s.v. *inland* 'land near a residence, land cultivated for the owner's use and not let to a tenant'.

SALT-HOUSE. *Salina* includes all kinds of salt workings from coastal pans to the boilers of Worcester and Cheshire. 'Salt-house' is the most comprehensive term.

ELc18 BELMESTHORPE PLOUGHS. See ELc 10.

WARNODE. See ELc 9 note.

ALFRED OF LINCOLN'S UFFINGTON. See DB Lincs. 27, 34-36.

ELc19 ARCHBISHOP ALDRED. Of York 1062-69.

TOPI'S SON. *Tope sune*, Anglo-Saxon instead of Latin *filius Topi*.

HARDWICK. The outlier is probably the Hardwick in Witchley; see DBL p.xl (Stenton) and p.227 (Foster and Longley).

ELe 1 KNOSSINGTON. Land here was included in Rutland in the time of Edward III, RH ii 50b.

APPENDIX

ALSTOE WAPENTAKE. Entries duplicated in Rutland and Lincolnshire. (Differences of substance are included, but those of phrasing are ignored.)

R 7 Market Overton and Stretton	ELc 11
Stretton, its outlier	Stretton
3 ploughs	3 ploughs in Lordship
Woodland, pasture in places	Woodland pasture
Value now £20	Value now £40
Alfred of Lincoln claims a fourth part, in Stretton	- - - -

R 8 Thistleton	ELc 12
Hugh	Hugh, the Countess' man

R 9 Thistleton	ELc 7
Alfred of Lincoln	Gleu, Alfred's man
Value before 1066, 20s; now 60s.	- - - -
- - - - - - -	Assessment in Witham

R 11 Whissendine	ELc 13
Double manor (see note)	Single manor
Hugh of Hotot	Hugh, the Countess' man
5 ploughs	5 ploughs in lordship
6 smallholders	7 smallholders
- - - - - - -	Meadow 10 furlongs long and 8 furlongs wide
Value before 1066 £8; now £13.	- - - -

R 12 Exton (No discrepancies)	ELc 14

R 13 Whitwell	ELc 15
Herbert	Herbert, the Countess' man
Woodland, pasture in places	Woodland pasture
Value before 1066, 20s; now 40(s). (see note)	Value 40s

R 15 Burley	ELc 5
Geoffrey, Gilbert of Ghent's man	Geoffrey, Gilbert's man
8 smallholders	7 smallholders
Woodland, pasture in places	Woodland

R 16 Ashwell	ELc 4
3 smallholders	2 smallholders

INDEX OF PERSONS

Familiar modern spellings are given when they exist. Unfamiliar names are usually given in an approximate late 11th century form, avoiding variants that were already obsolescent or pedantic. Spellings that mislead the modern eye are avoided where possible. Two, however, cannot be avoided: they are combined in the name of 'Leofgeat', pronounced 'Leffyet', or 'Levyet'. The definite article is omitted before bynames, except where there is reason to suppose that they described the individual. The chapter numbers of listed landholders are printed in italics.

Robert	EN 13;17
Robert of Tosny	EN 11
Robert Malet	3. R 10
Sasfrid	EN 12
Siward	R 9. ELc 6-7
Thorfrith	ELc 9
Topi, see Ulf	
Ulf	R 15. ELc 5
Ulf, Topi's son	ELc 19
Ungomar, see Oger	
Walter	EN 7-8
Earl Waltheof	R 7; 11-12. ELc 11; 13-14
William	EN 20
William, son of Ansculf	EN 13
William Peverel	EN 12

Churches and Clergy. **Abbey,** Peterborough EN 9-10. **Abbot** of Peterborough ELc 1;10;18, see Leofric. **Archbishop,** see Aldred. **Bishop** of Durham EN 6, of Lincoln EN 7-8. **Churches** ... All Saints (Stamford) EN 5. Hambleton R 19;21. Oakham R 17;21. St. Peter's (Stamford) R 21. ELc3. EN 5. **Clerk,** see Albert.

Secular Titles and Occupational Names. **Countess** *(comitissa)* ... Judith. **Earl** *(comes)* ... Harold, Morcar, Waltheof. **Queen** *(regina)* ... Edith.

INDEX OF PLACES

The name of each place is followed by (i) the initial of its Wapentake and its location on the map in this volume; (ii) its National Grid reference; (iii) the section reference in DB. Rutland is arranged by Wapentakes not by Landholders, so the numbers given beside the names in the list of Landholders are ignored, and the sections numbered continuously. Rutland places are preceded by R, places elsewhere are denoted by E. Bracketed figures denote mention in sections dealing with a different place. Unless otherwise stated in the notes, the identifications of VCH and the spellings of the Ordnance Survey are followed for places in England, of OEB for places abroad. Inverted commas mark lost places with known modern spelling; unidentified places are given in DB spelling in italics. The National Grid reference system is explained on all Ordnance Survey maps, and in the Automobile Association handbooks; the figures reading from left to right are given before those reading from bottom to top of the map. Places with grid references beginning with F are in the 100 kilometre grid square TF, with K are in SK, and with P in SP. Places with a bracketed grid reference do not appear on the current 1:50,000 maps. Places starred are not in Rutland, those marked LC being in Lincolnshire, and those marked LE in Leicestershire. All places belonging to Witchley Wapentake were in Northamptonshire in 1086. The Rutland Wapentakes are Alstoe (Northern Hundred An, Southern Hundred As), Martinsley (M) and Witchley (Wt).

	Map		Grid	Text
Ashwell	As	1	K86 13	R 16. ELc 4
'Awsthorp'	As	2	(K89 12)	R 14
Barrowden	Wt	1	K94 00	EN 2; 11
Belmesthorpe	Wt	2	F 04 10	EN 16. (ELc 10; 18)
*Bicker (LC)	-		-	ELc 17
Bisbrooke	Wt	3	P 88 99	EN 2; 17
Burley	As	3	K88 10	R 15. ELc 5
Caldecott	Wt	4	P 86 93	EN 7
Casterton	Wt	5	F 00 08	EN 4; 21
*Coleby (LC)	-		-	ELc 16
Cottesmore	An	1	K90 13	R 6
Empingham	Wt	6	K95 08	EN 12; 14 - 15
Essendine	Wt	7	F 04 12	EN 8
Exton	As	4	K92 11	R 12. ELc 14
Glaston	Wt	8	K89 00	EN 2; 20
Greetham	An	2	K92 14	R 5
Hambleton	M	1	K90 07	R 19; (21. ELc 3)
Hardwick	Wt	9	K96 12	ELc 19
Horn	Wt	10	K95 11	EN 6; 19
Ketton	Wt	11	K98 04	EN 1
*Knossington (LE)	M	2	K80 08	ELe 1
*Lavington (LC)	-		-	ELc 19
Luffenham	Wt	12	K93 03	EN 2 - 3; 20
Lyddington	Wt	13	P 87 97	EN 7
Morcott	Wt	14	K92 00	EN 2
Oakham	M	3	K86 08	R 17 - 18; (21. ELe 1)
Market Overton	An	3	K88 16	R 7. ELc 11; (16)
Portland	Wt	-	-	EN 5
Ridlington	M	4	K84 02	R 20
Ryhall	Wt	15	F 03 10	EN 16
'Sculthorp'	Wt	16	(K93 02)	EN 3
Seaton	Wt	17	P 90 98	EN 2; 11; 20
*Skillington (LC)	-		-	ELc 19

Places Not Named

In Martinsley Wapentake ... R 21.

Places Not in Rutland

Places indexed above are starred; for others, see Index of Persons.

Elsewhere in Britain

DURHAM Durham ... see Bishop. LEICESTER *Knossington. LINCOLN *Bicker; *Coleby; *Lavington; Lincoln ... see Alfred; *Skillington; *Stamford ... see also Churches; *Uffington; *Witham. NORTHAMPTON Peterborough ... see Abbey, Abbot.

Outside Britain

Cambrai ... see Godfrey. Ghent ... see Gilbert. Hotot ... see Hugh. Port ... see Hugh. Tosny ... see Robert.

MAP KEY

ALSTOE Northern Hundred (An)

1 Cottesmore
2 Greetham
3 Market Overton
4 Stretton
5 Teigh
6 Thistleton
7 Witham (LINCS)

ALSTOE Southern Hundred (As)

1 Ashwell
2 'Awsthorp'
3 Burley
4 Exton
5 Whissendine
6 Whitwell

MARTINSLEY (M)

1 Hambleton
2 Knossington (LEICS)
3 Oakham
4 Ridlington

S Stamford (LINCS)

WITCHLEY (Wt)

1 Barrowden
2 Belmesthorpe
3 Bisbrooke
4 Caldecott
5 Casterton
6 Empingham
7 Essendine
8 Glaston
9 Hardwick
10 Horn
11 Ketton
12 Luffenham
13 Lyddington
14 Morcott
   Portland
15 Ryhall
16 'Sculthorp'
17 Seaton
18 'Snelston'
19 Stoke Dry
20 Thorpe by Water
21 Tickencote
22 Tinwell
23 Tixover
24 Tolethorpe
25 Uffington (LINCS)

The pre-1974 County Boundary is marked on the map by thick lines; the Hundred boundaries by thin lines. In 1086 Witchley Wapentake was part of Northamptonshire.

National Grid 10-kilometre squares are shown on the map border.

Each four-figure grid square covers one square kilometre, or 247 acres, approximately 2 hides, at 120 acres to the hide.

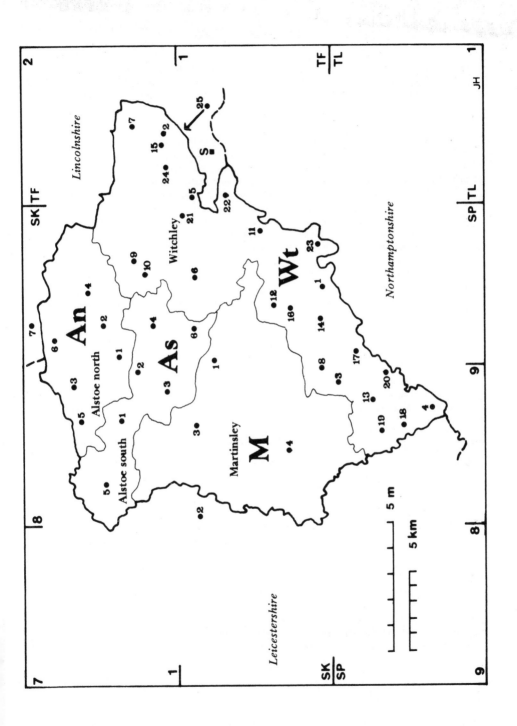

TECHNICAL TERMS

Many words meaning measurements have to be transliterated. But translation may not dodge other problems by the use of obsolete or made-up words which do not exist in modern English. The translations here used are given in italics. They cannot be exact; they aim at the nearest modern equivalent.

B. Marginal abbreviation for *Berewica*. (see below.) *B*

BEREWICA. An outlying place, attached to a manor. *o u t l i e r*

BORDARIUS. Cultivator of inferior status, usually with little land. *s m a l l h o l d e r*

BOVATA. A measure of land, usually an eighth of a *carucate*. *b o v a t e*

CARUCA. A plough, with the oxen that pulled it, usually reckoned at 8. *p l o u g h*

CARUCATA. Normally the equivalent of a hide in former Danish areas. *c a r u c a t e*

DOMINIUM. The mastery or dominion of a lord (*dominus*); including ploughs, land, men, villages *etc.*, reserved for the lord's use; often concentrated in a *home farm* or *demesne*, a 'Manor Farm' or 'Lordship Farm'. *l o r d s h i p*

GELDUM. The principal royal tax, originally levied during the Danish wars, normally at an equal number of pence on each *hide* of land. *t a x*

HIDA. A unit of land measurement, generally reckoned at 120 acres, but often different in practice; a measure of tax liability, often differing in number from the hides actually cultivated (see EN 1 note). *h i d e*

HUNDRED. A district within a Shire, whose assembly of notables and village representatives usually met about once a month. *H u n d r e d*

INLAND. Old English lord's land, usually exempt from tax, comparable with *dominium*. *i n l a n d*

LEUGA. A measure of length, probably about a mile and a half. (see R 6 note). *l e a g u e*

M. Marginal abbreviation for *manerium*, 'manor'. *M*

PERTICA. A measure of length, probably 16½ feet, a 40th of a furlong. (see R 13 note). *p e r c h*

PRAEPOSITUS, PRAEFECTUS. Old English *gerefa*, a royal officer. *r e e v e*

S. Marginal abbreviation for *soca*. (see below.) *S*

SACA. German *Sache*, English *sake*, Latin *causa*, 'affair', 'lawsuit'; the fullest authority normally exercised by a lord. *f u l l j u r i s d i c t i o n*

SOCA. 'soke', *socn* 'to seek' comparable with Latin *quaestio*. Jurisdiction, with the right to receive fines and a multiplicity of other dues. District in which such *soca* is exercised, a place in a *soca*. *j u r i s d i c t i o n*

SOCMANNUS. 'soke man', exercising, or subject to, jurisdiction; free from many villagers' burdens; before 1066 often with more land and higher status than villagers (see Middlesex, Bedfordshire appendices); bracketed in the Commissioners' brief with the *liber homo* 'free man'. *F r e e m a n*

T.R.E. *tempore regis Edwardi*, in King Edward's time. *b e f o r e 1 0 6 6*

VILLA. Translating Old English *tun*, town. The later distinction between a small *village* and a large *town* was not yet in use in 1086. *v i l l a g e* or *t o w n*

VILLANUS. Member of a *villa*, usually with more land than a *bordarius*. *v i l l a g e r*

VIRGATA. A fraction of a *hide*, usually a quarter, notionally 30 acres. *v i r g a t e*

WAPENTAC. Equivalent of the English Hundred in former Danish areas. *W a p e n t a k e*

SYSTEMS OF REFERENCE TO DOMESDAY BOOK

The manuscript is divided into numbered chapters, and the chapters into sections, usually marked by large initials and red ink. Farley however did not number the sections. References have therefore been inexact, by folio numbers, which cannot be closer than an entire page or column. Moreover, half a dozen different ways of referring to the same column have been devised. In 1816 Ellis used three separate systems in his indices; (i) on pages i - cvii; 435-518; 537-570; (ii) on pages 1-144; (iii) on pages 145-433 and 519-535. Other systems have since come into use, notably that used by Vinogradoff, here followed. This edition numbers the sections, the normal practicable form of close reference; but since all discussion of Domesday for three hundred years has been obliged to refer to page or column, a comparative table will help to locate references given. The five columns below give Vinogradoff's notation, Ellis' three systems, and that employed by Welldon Finn and others. Maitland, Stenton, Darby and others have usually followed Ellis (i).

Vinogradoff	Ellis (i)	Ellis (ii)	Ellis (iii)	Finn
152 a	152	152 a	152	152 ai
152 b	152	152 a	152.2	152 a2
152 c	152 b	152 b	152 b	152 bi
152 d	152 b	152 b	152 b2	152 b2

In Rutland, the relation between the Vinogradoff column notation, here followed, and the chapters and sections is:

280 d	Landholders (with Notts.)
. . . .	
293 c	R 1-12
293 d	R 12-20
294 a	R 21